UNDERSTANDING CYBER THREATS THROUGH BEHAVIORAL INTELLIGENCE

Taiwo Osiyemi

Understanding Cyber Threats Through Behavioral Intelligence

Published in Nigeria in 2021 by Plexity Digital

A catalogue record of this book will be available from the National Library of Nigeria.

TABLE OF CONTENTS

PREFACE

Cyber threats rarely announce themselves. They arrive quietly, disguised as normal activity, routine access, or minor system irregularities that seem harmless in isolation. By the time an organization recognizes that something is wrong, the damage has often already begun. This book was written from the belief that cybersecurity must move beyond reaction and begin with understanding. Not understanding tools or alerts alone, but understanding behavior.

Over the years, cybersecurity conversations have been dominated by breaches, exploits, malware variants, and defensive products. While these elements matter, they often distract from a more fundamental truth. Attacks succeed not only because systems are weak, but because early behavioral signals are ignored, misunderstood, or buried under noise. Long before a system is compromised, it usually exhibits patterns that suggest probing, testing, learning, and gradual manipulation. These patterns are behavioral, not technical in the narrow sense, and they form the foundation of what this book refers to as behavioral intelligence.

This book emerged from sustained engagement with complex digital environments where risk is constant and visibility is limited. In such environments, the difference between stability and failure is rarely a single control or configuration. It is the ability to recognize intent through patterns. Behavioral intelligence is not about predicting the future with certainty. It is about increasing awareness early enough to intervene meaningfully. It shifts the focus from asking what happened to asking what is forming.

Nigeria and many other fast growing digital economies face a unique challenge. Digital systems are expanding rapidly across finance, telecommunications, public services, education, and healthcare. These systems are increasingly central to daily life, yet the security frameworks supporting them often remain reactive. There is heavy investment in tools, but less attention to interpretation. Logs are collected, alerts are generated, dashboards are filled, yet understanding remains fragmented. This gap between data and meaning is where behavioral intelligence becomes essential.

The purpose of this book is not to dismiss existing security practices, but to reframe them. It argues that cybersecurity maturity is not defined by how quickly an organization responds to incidents, but by how early it recognizes risk. Behavior is the earliest expression of intent in digital systems. Attackers behave before they act. Users behave before they make mistakes. Systems behave before they fail. When these behaviors are observed, correlated, and interpreted correctly, they offer a powerful opportunity for prevention.

This book also responds to a broader concern. Cybersecurity is too often treated as a technical silo, isolated from organizational decision making and national strategy. In reality, digital security influences trust, economic stability, institutional credibility, and public confidence. A compromised financial system affects livelihoods. A breached government platform affects governance. A disrupted infrastructure affects national resilience. Understanding cyber threats through behavioral intelligence is therefore not only a technical discipline, but a strategic responsibility.

Throughout this book, readers will encounter an approach that prioritizes clarity over complexity. Behavioral intelligence does not require perfect data or flawless systems. It requires disciplined observation, contextual awareness, and the willingness to ask better questions. Why is this access pattern changing. Why is this system behaving differently under similar conditions. Why is this alert recurring without escalation. These questions, when asked consistently, reshape how security teams operate and how organizations understand risk.

The chapters that follow are structured to build understanding gradually. They begin by challenging assumptions about how attacks start and why reactive models persist. They move into the mechanics of behavior, correlation, and interpretation. They explore the role of artificial intelligence not as a replacement for human judgment, but as a support for it. They examine how behavioral intelligence applies across industries, from banking and telecommunications to government systems and cloud platforms. Finally, they look ahead to a future where adaptive threats demand adaptive thinking.

This book is written for cybersecurity professionals, analysts, engineers, decision makers, and policymakers. It is also written for those who may not work directly in security, but whose organizations depend on digital systems to function. Behavioral intelligence is not an advanced concept reserved for specialists. It is a mindset that can be cultivated wherever systems interact with people and data.

There is a temptation in technology to chase novelty. New tools promise better detection, faster response, and broader coverage. While innovation is necessary, it must be grounded in understanding. Behavioral intelligence reminds us that the most valuable insights often come from patterns we already have access to, if only we learn how to see them. It encourages patience in a field driven by urgency, and depth in a space crowded by surface level metrics.

Writing this book was motivated by a simple but urgent question. How many cyber incidents could be prevented if organizations learned to recognize what was forming rather than reacting to what had already happened. The answer, while not easily quantified, points toward a more resilient digital future.

If this book succeeds, it will not be because it introduces a new framework or terminology, but because it helps readers think differently about what they already see. Cybersecurity does not begin with alarms. It begins with awareness. Behavioral intelligence is the discipline of paying attention early, interpreting wisely, and acting before harm becomes inevitable.

This is the foundation upon which the rest of this book is built.

FOREWORD

Digital systems now sit at the center of modern life. They mediate how money moves, how governments operate, how businesses scale, and how societies communicate. As these systems expand, so does the surface on which risk appears. Yet much of the global conversation on cybersecurity still treats threat as an event rather than a process. We talk about breaches after they occur, vulnerabilities after they are exploited, and damage after trust has already been lost. This book enters that conversation with a necessary shift in perspective.

Understanding Cyber Threats Through Behavioral Intelligence argues that security is not first a question of tools, but of interpretation. It challenges readers to reconsider how threats develop, how systems signal distress, and how human and machine behavior often reveal intent long before consequences materialize. This is a timely contribution, particularly for countries navigating rapid digital growth without the luxury of stable legacy infrastructure or unlimited security resources.

One of the strengths of this book lies in its refusal to dramatize cybersecurity. There is no attempt to sensationalize attackers or inflate technological complexity. Instead, the author focuses on something more difficult and more valuable: disciplined observation. Behavioral intelligence, as presented here, is not a speculative concept. It is grounded in how systems actually behave under pressure and how attackers, users, and platforms leave traces through patterns rather than announcements.

For Nigeria and other fast growing digital economies, this perspective is especially important. Financial systems, identity platforms, telecommunications networks, and public service applications are scaling at unprecedented speed. In many cases, security frameworks are implemented after deployment, not during design. This creates environments where data is abundant, alerts are frequent, and understanding is scarce. The result is not necessarily insecurity in the obvious sense, but fragility. Systems appear stable until they are not.

This book makes a compelling case that fragility often begins with misread behavior. Repeated access attempts that are dismissed as user error. Small configuration changes that go unexplained. Network movements that seem benign in isolation. These are not anomalies to be filtered out. They are signals to be interpreted. Behavioral intelligence gives security teams and decision makers a language for understanding these signals before they combine into failure.

What also distinguishes this work is its treatment of artificial intelligence. Rather than presenting AI as a solution in itself, the author positions it as a support mechanism for human judgment. This is an important correction. In many organizations, automation has been adopted as a substitute for thinking rather than an aid to it. The book reminds us that intelligence without context can amplify confusion rather than resolve it. Behavioral models are only as useful as the questions they are designed to answer.

From an industry perspective, this book speaks directly to practitioners who are exhausted by noise. Security operations centers are flooded with alerts, dashboards, and metrics, yet meaningful prioritization remains elusive. Behavioral intelligence offers a way to reduce that burden by shifting attention from volume to relevance. It encourages teams to focus on sequences rather than events and intent rather than indicators. This approach has practical implications for incident prevention, response efficiency, and organizational confidence.

From a national perspective, the implications are even broader. Cybersecurity is no longer confined to enterprise risk. It affects public trust, economic continuity, and institutional legitimacy. A compromised payment system disrupts commerce. A breached government database undermines confidence. A prolonged outage weakens social stability. In this context, the ability to understand threats early becomes a matter of public interest. Behavioral intelligence supports that ability by making risk visible before it becomes disruptive.

The author also makes an important contribution by connecting technical decisions to long term consequences. Security failures are often treated as isolated incidents. This book frames them as symptoms of deeper interpretive gaps. When organizations do not understand their systems, they cannot protect them. When nations do not invest in security literacy, they inherit vulnerability. These are not abstract claims. They are observations drawn from real environments where digital systems are expected to carry increasing social and economic weight.

This work will be valuable to a wide audience. Cybersecurity professionals will find in it a framework that clarifies what they already sense but struggle to articulate. Executives and policymakers will gain insight into why security investments sometimes fail to produce confidence. Technologists and data scientists will encounter a reminder that intelligence is not measured by complexity, but by usefulness. Students and early career professionals will be introduced to cybersecurity as a field that rewards patience, curiosity, and disciplined thinking.

Perhaps most importantly, this book encourages responsibility without alarmism. It does not argue that all threats can be prevented or that systems can be made perfect. It argues instead for attentiveness. For learning to recognize when something is changing and asking why. In an environment defined by uncertainty, that skill may be the most valuable form of defense.

As digital systems continue to shape the future of governance, commerce, and social interaction, the need for thoughtful security frameworks will only grow. This book contributes meaningfully to that need. It invites readers to slow down, observe carefully, and think deeply about what digital behavior reveals.

In doing so, it reframes cybersecurity not as a race to respond, but as a discipline of understanding. That shift, if taken seriously, has the potential to strengthen organizations, industries, and nations alike.

INTRODUCTION

Cyber threats do not begin with disruption. They begin with behavior. Long before systems fail, data is exposed, or operations are interrupted, there are small changes in how digital environments are used, accessed, and navigated. These changes often appear ordinary. A login attempt that happens at an unusual time. A system request that repeats without escalation. A pattern of access that slowly drifts from the norm. Individually, such events are easy to dismiss. Together, they form the earliest language of cyber risk.

This book begins from a simple observation. Most organizations do not lack data about their systems. They lack understanding. Logs are collected, alerts are generated, dashboards are populated, yet breaches continue to occur. The issue is not always the absence of controls or technology. It is the failure to interpret behavior early enough to act meaningfully. Understanding cyber threats through behavioral intelligence is an attempt to close that gap.

Traditional cybersecurity models have been built around events. An intrusion is detected. An alert is triggered. A response is initiated. This model assumes that threats are sudden and visible. In reality, many modern attacks are gradual and adaptive. Attackers study systems over time. They test boundaries quietly. They learn how users behave, how controls respond, and where oversight is weakest. By the time an alert signals compromise, the attacker may already be embedded. Behavioral intelligence shifts attention from the moment of attack to the period of formation that precedes it.

Behavior in digital systems is never random. Users behave in patterns. Systems respond in predictable ways. Attackers adapt based on feedback. When these behaviors are observed in isolation, they appear unremarkable. When they are correlated across time, context, and systems, they reveal intent. Behavioral intelligence is the practice of identifying, connecting, and interpreting these patterns before harm occurs. It is not a replacement for existing security controls. It is the lens through which those controls become meaningful.

The need for this approach is especially urgent in environments experiencing rapid digital growth. Nigeria, like many emerging digital economies, is expanding its use of technology across finance, telecommunications, public administration, education, healthcare, and commerce. Digital platforms now support essential services that affect millions of people daily. As reliance on these systems grows, so does the impact of failure. Cybersecurity in this context is not only a technical concern. It is a matter of economic stability, institutional trust, and public confidence.

Despite this reality, security practices often remain reactive. Investment is directed toward tools that promise faster detection or broader coverage. While such tools are valuable, they do not automatically produce understanding. Security teams are frequently overwhelmed by volume. Alerts compete for attention. Prioritization becomes difficult. Fatigue sets in. In this environment, early behavioral signals are easily missed. The result is a cycle of late detection and rushed response.

This book challenges that cycle. It argues that cybersecurity maturity is not defined by how quickly an organization reacts, but by how early it recognizes risk. Behavior is the earliest expression of intent in digital systems. When behavior changes, something is forming. Behavioral intelligence teaches us to ask why before asking what to do. It encourages curiosity before urgency. It places interpretation at the center of defense.

A key theme throughout this book is context. Behavior has meaning only when understood within its environment. A failed login attempt may be benign in one context and suspicious in another. Network traffic may be expected during peak usage and concerning during quiet periods. Behavioral intelligence requires an understanding of normal activity, not as a static baseline, but as a living pattern that evolves. This makes the discipline both challenging and powerful. It demands attention to detail and respect for complexity.

Artificial intelligence plays an important role in this process, but it is not the starting point. Machine learning models can assist in identifying patterns and correlations across large datasets. They can surface anomalies and prioritize signals. However, without context and human judgment, automation can amplify noise rather than reduce it. This book treats artificial intelligence as a support mechanism rather than a solution in itself. Behavioral intelligence depends on asking the right questions, not simply processing more data.

Another central argument of this book is that behavioral intelligence is not limited to cybersecurity specialists. While technical expertise is essential, the interpretation of behavior benefits from diverse perspectives. System administrators, developers, analysts, managers, and policymakers all interact with digital systems differently. Each perspective contributes to a more complete understanding of how systems are used and misused. Security improves when interpretation is shared rather than sold.

The chapters that follow are structured to build this understanding step by step. The early chapters challenge common assumptions about how attacks begin and why reactive models persist. They introduce behavior as the primary signal of risk and explore how meaning emerges from correlation. Later chapters examine how attackers adapt over time, how artificial intelligence can be applied responsibly, and how prediction changes the economics of defense. Industry specific discussions illustrate how behavioral intelligence applies across different sectors. The final chapter looks ahead to a future where adaptability is the defining feature of both threats and defenses.

Throughout the book, emphasis is placed on practicality. Behavioral intelligence is not presented as an abstract theory. It is a discipline shaped by real environments, real constraints, and real consequences. Examples are drawn from contexts where security decisions affect financial stability, service continuity, and public trust. The goal is not to overwhelm readers with technical detail, but to equip them with a way of thinking that can be applied regardless of role or industry.

This book is written for those who are responsible for digital systems and those who depend on them. It speaks to cybersecurity professionals seeking clarity amid complexity. It addresses executives and decision makers who must balance risk, cost, and confidence. It invites policymakers to consider security as part of national capability rather than operational overhead. It also welcomes students and early career professionals who want to understand cybersecurity beyond tools and tactics.

At its core, this book makes a modest claim. Most cyber threats can be better understood if we learn to pay attention earlier. Behavioral intelligence does not promise perfect security. No system is immune to failure. What it offers is the ability to recognize risk while there is still time to act. It turns defense from a race against damage into a practice of awareness.

Cybersecurity does not begin with alarms. It begins with observation. It matures through interpretation. It succeeds through timely action. Understanding cyber threats through behavioral intelligence is an invitation to adopt this progression. The chapters ahead explore what that adoption requires and what it makes possible.

CHAPTER 1

Why Cyber Attacks Rarely Begin with an Attack

Cyber-attacks are often described as sudden, disruptive events. A system is breached, data is exposed, services are interrupted, and attention immediately shifts to response and recovery. This framing, while common, obscures how most incidents actually develop. In reality, cyber-attacks rarely begin with a single decisive action. They emerge gradually, shaped by patterns of behavior that evolve quietly within digital environments long before any visible damage occurs. Understanding this distinction is essential, because it determines whether security efforts focus on reaction or recognition.

Digital systems operate through continuous interaction. Users authenticate, request access, perform tasks, and move between resources. Applications exchange data with other services, devices communicate automatically, and background processes run without human intervention. Over time, these interactions form stable behavioral patterns that reflect legitimate use. When those patterns begin to change, even slightly, it often indicates that something in the environment is shifting. These changes are not always malicious, but they are rarely meaningless. Behavior is the earliest expression of risk, long before it manifests as a technical violation.

Modern attackers understand this dynamic and exploit it deliberately. Instead of relying on forceful entry or obvious exploitation, many threat actors begin by observing how systems respond. They test boundaries carefully, adjusting their behavior based on feedback. They attempt logins at varying times, explore permissions without exceeding them, and interact with systems in ways that mimic legitimate users or administrators. This phase is not designed to cause disruption. Its purpose is to learn. By studying system behavior, attackers identify blind spots, trust assumptions, and areas where oversight is weak.

During this early phase, behavior is the only signal available. There may be no malware, no data exfiltration, and no policy violations. Each individual action appears normal enough to avoid concern. A failed login attempt is logged and forgotten. A successful login raises no alarm. A resource is accessed within allowed permissions. Viewed independently, none of these actions justify intervention. Viewed together over time, they often reveal intent. Behavioral intelligence depends on recognizing this accumulation of meaning.

Traditional security models struggle to detect this stage because they are built around discrete events rather than evolving patterns. Alerts are triggered when thresholds are crossed, signatures are matched, or rules are violated. This approach is effective for detecting known threats, but it is poorly suited to recognizing gradual formation. By treating each event as isolated, security systems lose the context necessary to interpret behavior. The result is a focus on incidents rather than trajectories.

The complexity of modern digital environments amplifies this problem. Organizations now operate across hybrid infrastructures that include on premises systems, cloud platforms, mobile endpoints, application interfaces, and third party services. Each layer introduces new interactions and generates large volumes of data. Within this volume, meaningful behavioral changes are easily buried. Attackers exploit this noise by blending in, behaving just closely enough to normal patterns to avoid scrutiny while slowly advancing their objectives.

Credential based attacks illustrate this challenge clearly. When attackers obtain valid credentials through phishing, reuse, or social engineering, they no longer need to bypass technical controls. They enter systems as legitimate users. Many security tools treat authenticated access as trustworthy by default. The attack proceeds not through exploitation, but through misuse. Access patterns shift gradually, permissions are explored carefully, and lateral movement resembles administrative activity. Without behavioral context, these actions appear acceptable until significant damage has already occurred.

Behavior also plays a central role in insider related incidents. Not all insider threats are intentional. Many originate from convenience driven behavior that deviates slowly from policy. Passwords are reused, access is shared, controls are bypassed to save time. These behaviors create conditions that external attackers later exploit. Again, the threat does not begin with an attack. It begins with behavior that erodes boundaries over time.

Systems themselves contribute to this dynamic. Applications, services, and automated processes exhibit behavior that can change in response to configuration drift, misuse, or compromise. A service account that begins accessing resources outside its typical scope may still operate within allowed permissions, yet its behavior has changed meaningfully. A server that increases communication with an external endpoint may not violate policy, but it may indicate data leakage in progress. Without behavioral baselines and context, these changes are easy to overlook.

Recognizing that cyber-attacks rarely begin with an attack also reframes how prevention is understood. Prevention is often equated with blocking unauthorized actions at the moment they occur. Firewalls, authentication mechanisms, and endpoint protection all serve this purpose. These controls are necessary, but they operate at the point of violation. Behavioral intelligence operates earlier. It seeks to understand when something is becoming unsafe, not when it has already crossed a line.

Adopting this approach requires more than new tools. It requires a shift in mindset. Many organizations reward response rather than anticipation. Incident response metrics focus on how quickly breaches are contained, not on how early risk is recognized. This reinforces a culture where attacks are treated as inevitable events rather than preventable processes. Behavioral intelligence challenges this assumption by suggesting that many incidents are not sudden, but unnoticed.

Data structure and analysis practices also play a role. Logs are typically designed for auditing and compliance, not for interpretation. They record what happened, not why it matters. Behavioral intelligence requires correlation across time, systems, and identities. It requires understanding how actions relate to one another and how patterns evolve. This often demands changes in how data is collected, stored, and reviewed, as well as how analysts are trained to think.

From a leadership perspective, this understanding alters the questions that matter. Asking whether a system is secure implies a static condition. Behavioral intelligence reframes security as a continuous assessment of change. It asks how systems are behaving today compared to yesterday, and whether that behavior is drifting in ways that increase risk. This perspective supports earlier intervention and more informed decision making.

At a national level, the implications are significant. As digital infrastructure underpins essential services, failures often trace back to systems that exhibited warning signs long before disruption occurred. Financial instability, service outages, and loss of public trust frequently follow periods of unnoticed behavioral change. Behavioral intelligence offers a way to surface these signals while there is still time to respond thoughtfully.

1.1 Early Signals That Are Commonly Misread or Ignored

One of the most persistent reasons cyber-attacks progress unnoticed is not the absence of signals, but the way those signals are interpreted. In many environments, early behavioral indicators are present and even logged, yet they are dismissed as operational noise, user error, or harmless anomalies. This misinterpretation is rarely due to negligence. It is often the result of organizational habits that prioritize stability over curiosity and continuity over questioning. When systems appear to be functioning, there is little incentive to look closely at subtle change.

A common example is repeated authentication irregularities that do not cross enforcement thresholds. An account may experience a steady increase in failed login attempts spread across long intervals. Because these attempts do not trigger lockouts or alerts, they are treated as forgetfulness or network issues. Over time, successful logins begin to appear at slightly unusual hours, still within acceptable policy. Individually, each event is defensible. Collectively, they may indicate credential testing and eventual compromise. Without behavioral correlation, this progression remains invisible.

Another frequently ignored signal is gradual expansion of access usage. An account may begin accessing resources it has permission to use but has historically never touched. Because no rule is violated, the activity is allowed. Behavioral intelligence treats this as meaningful change. It asks why access patterns are shifting and what conditions enabled the shift. In contrast, event based security models often treat permitted access as inherently safe.

System to system behavior is also commonly overlooked. Services may begin communicating more frequently, querying different endpoints, or exchanging data volumes outside historical norms. These changes are often attributed to updates, growth, or temporary load. While such explanations may be valid, behavioral intelligence insists on verification. It recognizes that attackers often exploit trusted system relationships precisely because they attract less scrutiny.

The challenge is compounded by alert fatigue. Security teams are often overwhelmed by volume and prioritize clear violations over ambiguous change. This creates an environment where subtle signals are filtered out by design. Behavioral intelligence requires resisting this impulse. It encourages organizations to treat ambiguity as a prompt for investigation rather than a reason for dismissal.

These early signals rarely indicate certainty. They indicate possibility. Behavioral intelligence does not demand immediate response to every deviation. It demands awareness, tracking, and contextual understanding. This distinction is critical. The goal is not to stop systems at the first sign of change, but to understand whether that change is forming a trajectory toward risk.

Case Study One: Gradual Credential Misuse in a Financial Services Environment

In a large financial services organization, an internal application supported daily operations for hundreds of staff across multiple departments. Access was role based, and authentication logs were routinely collected for compliance purposes. Over several weeks, a service account associated with a back office function began exhibiting subtle changes in behavior.

Login attempts increased slightly outside normal operating hours. Resource access expanded beyond historical patterns, though still within assigned permissions. None of these actions violated policy.

Because the account continued to authenticate successfully and no alerts were triggered, the activity was not escalated. Analysts reviewing daily logs focused on more obvious issues such as repeated failed logins on user accounts and external scanning attempts. The service account activity was considered low risk.

Several weeks later, anomalous financial adjustments were detected. Investigation revealed that the service account credentials had been compromised through a third party integration. The attacker had spent weeks learning system behavior, identifying which actions attracted attention and which did not. By the time the fraudulent activity occurred, the attacker had a clear understanding of operational patterns.

A retrospective analysis showed that the earliest signs of compromise were present nearly a month before impact. The gradual shift in access times, the expansion of resource usage, and the increase in authentication frequency were all recorded. What was missing was interpretation. The organization had data, but it lacked behavioral context. The signals were treated as acceptable variance rather than emerging risk.

Following the incident, the organization revised its approach. Instead of reviewing authentication events in isolation, analysts began tracking behavior over time. Baselines were established for service accounts, and deviations were flagged for review rather than dismissal. This did not eliminate incidents entirely, but it significantly reduced the time between early signal and intervention.

1.2 How System Behavior Reveals Risk Before Users Do

While much attention is placed on user activity, some of the most revealing early indicators of cyber risk come from systems themselves. Applications, services, and automated processes develop consistent behavioral patterns over time. They communicate at predictable intervals, exchange familiar data volumes, and interact with known endpoints. When these patterns change without a clear operational reason, systems are often signaling distress long before users are affected or attackers make themselves visible.

System behavior is frequently treated as background activity. Automated traffic is expected. Service to service communication is assumed to be trustworthy. When volumes increase or patterns shift, the explanation is often attributed to growth, updates, or temporary load. While these explanations may be accurate, they are also convenient. Behavioral intelligence insists that such assumptions be tested rather than accepted by default. It treats unexplained change as information rather than inconvenience.

Attackers understand the protective value of trusted system relationships. Compromising a service account or internal application allows them to move quietly, often without triggering alarms designed for user facing activity. Once inside, attackers observe how systems communicate, which connections are monitored, and which actions generate alerts. They adapt their behavior to blend into existing patterns, gradually extending their reach.

One of the most overlooked signals in this context is frequency drift. A system may begin communicating more often than usual, or at different times, without exceeding predefined thresholds. Another signal is destination drift, where systems begin interacting with new endpoints that are technically allowed but historically unused. Data volume changes also matter. Gradual increases in outbound traffic may not violate policy, but they can indicate data collection or staging activity.

Because these changes often occur slowly, they are easy to rationalize. Security teams may assume legitimate operational causes, especially when no immediate failure is visible. Behavioral intelligence encourages a different response. It does not assume malicious intent, but it demands explanation. It asks why behavior is changing and whether that change aligns with known operational shifts.

This approach requires historical understanding. Without knowledge of how systems normally behave, deviation cannot be recognized. Behavioral baselining becomes essential. This does not mean rigid profiles that fail under change. It means living baselines that evolve while still preserving memory. Systems should be allowed to grow and adapt, but growth should be visible and explainable.

Case Study Two: Silent Data Exposure Through Trusted System Channels

A technology enabled public service organization operated several internal applications that exchanged data with a central repository. These systems handled sensitive records and were integrated with external vendors for reporting and analytics. Communication between systems was encrypted and authenticated, and access controls were considered robust. From a traditional security perspective, the environment appeared well protected.

Over time, one internal application began increasing its outbound data transfers during off peak hours. The increase was gradual and remained within acceptable bandwidth limits. No alerts were generated. Because the application had permission to communicate with the repository and external analytics endpoints, the activity was considered normal. The organization was also experiencing growth, which made the increase appear reasonable.

Months later, a routine audit uncovered discrepancies in how data was being stored externally. Further investigation revealed that the internal application had been compromised through a vulnerable third party library. The attacker had gained access to the application environment and used existing system connections to extract data slowly over time. Because the data moved through trusted channels and followed allowed paths, traditional monitoring did not flag it.

A post incident review revealed that system behavior had changed significantly well before the discovery. Communication frequency had increased. Data transfer timing had shifted. New external endpoints had been introduced gradually. Each change was recorded in logs, but none were correlated or questioned. The organization had visibility, but not interpretation.

In response, the organization implemented behavioral monitoring for system activity. Instead of focusing solely on access permissions, they began tracking how systems behaved relative to historical patterns. Changes in frequency, destination, and data volume were reviewed for context. When behavior shifted, teams sought operational explanations rather than assuming legitimacy.

This shift did not require replacing existing security controls. It required reframing how system behavior was understood. Over time, the organization developed a clearer picture of normal operations and a faster path to questioning abnormal ones. The result was earlier detection of misconfiguration, misuse, and compromise.

This case reinforces a critical lesson. Systems speak through behavior just as users do. When their behavior changes, they are communicating something important. Behavioral intelligence teaches organizations to listen before failure makes the message unavoidable.

With this understanding, the foundation is set for exploring how these behavioral signals can be systematically interpreted, correlated, and acted upon without overwhelming security teams.

CHAPTER 2

Behavior as the First Language of Digital Risk

Every digital system speaks. It speaks through actions, responses, timing, repetition, and deviation. These expressions form a language that exists before alerts, before failures, and before damage. Behavior is the first language of digital risk, and learning to understand it is fundamental to effective cybersecurity. While tools record events and controls enforce rules, behavior reveals intent. It shows how users, systems, and attackers interact with their environment over time.

In many organizations, security conversations begin with indicators. Indicators of compromise, indicators of attack, indicators of malware. These indicators are useful, but they are often late. They describe what has already crossed a known boundary. Behavioral intelligence begins earlier. It focuses on how boundaries are approached, tested, and reshaped. It recognizes that intent is rarely expressed in a single action. It is expressed through consistency, adaptation, and gradual change.

Digital behavior emerges from repetition. Users tend to access the same systems, at similar times, using familiar paths. Applications communicate in predictable cycles. Services request and deliver data according to established workflows. Over time, these patterns form a baseline that reflects normal operation. Risk appears when behavior begins to drift from this baseline without a clear explanation. The drift may be subtle, but it is rarely accidental.

Understanding behavior as a language requires abandoning the idea that security signals must be loud to be meaningful. In fact, the most important signals are often quiet. They do not violate rules. They do not trigger alerts. They simply differ. Behavioral intelligence treats difference as information. It does not immediately label it as malicious, but it does not ignore it either. It asks what the difference represents and whether it is consistent with known change.

One of the reasons behaviors is such a powerful signal is that it is difficult to fake consistently. Attackers can imitate individual actions, but sustaining imitation over time without deviation is challenging. Legitimate users behave with familiarity and purpose. Attackers behave with exploration and uncertainty. Even when they use valid credentials, their interaction patterns often reveal hesitation, testing, and adjustment. Behavioral intelligence looks for these subtle mismatches.

Another important aspect of behavioral language is sequence. Single events rarely tell a story. Sequences do. A login followed by access to an unusual resource, followed by data queries at irregular intervals, followed by increased system interaction during quiet periods forms a narrative. Each action alone is defensible. Together, they suggest intent. Behavioral intelligence is the discipline of reading these narratives rather than reacting to isolated sentences.

This approach also changes how anomalies are understood. Traditional security models often treat anomalies as errors to be filtered out. False positives are reduced by narrowing thresholds and suppressing noise. Behavioral intelligence takes a different view. It treats anomalies as questions rather than problems. An anomaly asks why something is different. It invites investigation rather than dismissal. This does not mean chasing every irregularity. It means tracking irregularities that persist or evolve.

Context is central to this process. Behavior cannot be interpreted without understanding the environment in which it occurs. A change in access patterns during a system upgrade may be expected. The same change during a period of stability may be concerning. Behavioral intelligence relies on contextual awareness. It requires collaboration between security teams, operations teams, and business units to explain legitimate change and identify unexplained drift.

The language of behavior also applies to systems, not just people. Applications exhibit behavioral signatures. Services have rhythms. Automated processes follow schedules. When these behaviors change, systems are signaling something. Configuration drift, misuse, compromise, or unintended interaction can all manifest as behavioral change. Recognizing this requires treating systems as active participants in security rather than passive assets.

One of the most challenging aspects of behavioral intelligence is patience. Behavior unfolds over time. It requires observation across days, weeks, or months. In fast paced environments, there is pressure to act quickly and move on. Behavioral intelligence asks teams to slow down just enough to see patterns form. This is not a call for inaction. It is a call for informed action.

Artificial intelligence can assist in this process by identifying correlations that are difficult for humans to detect manually. Machine learning models can surface patterns across large datasets, highlight deviations, and prioritize signals. However, these tools are only effective when guided by behavioral understanding. Without context, automation can amplify noise. Behavioral intelligence ensures that technology serves interpretation rather than replacing it.

Another benefit of treating behavior as the first language of risk is its applicability across environments. Whether in finance, telecommunications, healthcare, government systems, or cloud platforms, behavior remains consistent as a signal. Technologies change. Threats evolve. Behavior persists. This makes behavioral intelligence a durable framework rather than a transient technique.

Organizational culture plays a significant role in whether behavioral signals are recognized. In environments where questioning is discouraged and stability is prioritized over understanding; behavioral drift is often ignored. In contrast, organizations that encourage curiosity and explanation are better positioned to detect risk early. Behavioral intelligence thrives in cultures that value learning over blame.

Leadership support is also critical. When executives view security as a compliance requirement, behavioral analysis is seen as unnecessary complexity. When security is viewed as a strategic capability, behavioral intelligence becomes an asset. Leaders who ask how systems are behaving create space for early discussion and intervention. Those who ask only whether systems are secure often receive incomplete answers.

Digital systems underpin essential services. When behavioral drift goes unnoticed, failures can cascade across sectors. Early recognition of risk supports resilience. It allows institutions to adapt before disruption occurs. Behavioral intelligence thus contributes to national stability by extending the window for response.

2.1 Behavior as a Continuous Signal Rather Than an Isolated Event

A persistent weakness in many cybersecurity strategies is the tendency to treat risk as something that appears suddenly and decisively. This way of thinking encourages organizations to design systems that wait for clear violations before responding. Alerts are configured to trigger when thresholds are crossed, rules are broken, or signatures are matched. While this approach is useful for detecting known threats, it overlooks how most risk actually develops. Behavior does not arrive in a single moment. It unfolds gradually, shaped by repetition, adjustment, and accumulation over time.

When behavior is understood as a continuous signal, attention shifts from individual actions to movement and direction. A single failed login, a one-time access anomaly, or an isolated configuration change rarely tells a meaningful story on its own. Behavioral intelligence asks whether such actions are part of a broader pattern. Is the frequency increasing. Is the timing changing. Is the scope expanding. These questions help security teams detect drift long before a system reaches a point of failure. The emphasis moves away from reacting to incidents and toward understanding trajectories.

This perspective also challenges the notion of a fixed baseline. In dynamic environments, normal behavior is not static. Systems evolve, users adapt, and workloads change. Behavioral intelligence recognizes that normality is contextual and time dependent. Rather than relying on rigid thresholds that quickly become obsolete, it encourages continuous observation and recalibration. Behavior is assessed relative to recent history, operational context, and environmental change. This flexibility makes behavioral analysis more resilient in environments characterized by growth and transformation.

Viewing behavior as continuous also helps organizations manage uncertainty more effectively. Not every deviation is dangerous, and not every change requires intervention. Behavioral intelligence does not demand immediate action at the first sign of difference. Instead, it promotes sustained attention. It encourages teams to track how behavior evolves, whether it stabilizes, reverses, or accelerates. This measured approach reduces unnecessary disruption while preserving the ability to act early when risk becomes clearer.

Over time, this way of thinking transforms security operations. Teams become less dependent on alerts and more attuned to patterns. They develop a sense of how their systems normally behave and how that behavior shifts under different conditions. This familiarity is difficult to automate, but it is essential. Behavioral intelligence turns security from a series of reactions into a continuous practice of observation and interpretation.

2.2 The Role of Intent in Interpreting Digital Behavior

Behavior becomes meaningful when it is interpreted through intent. Digital actions are not random. They are performed with purpose, whether that purpose is legitimate, accidental, or malicious. Traditional security models often focus on whether an action is allowed rather than why it is occurring. Behavioral intelligence reverses this emphasis. It seeks to understand motivation by examining how actions relate to one another over time.

Intent rarely reveals itself through a single decision. It emerges through repetition, adjustment, and response to feedback. Legitimate users typically behave with confidence and familiarity. They know which systems they need, which resources are relevant, and how to complete their tasks efficiently. Their behavior tends to be consistent, even when workloads fluctuate. Attackers, by contrast, often display exploratory behavior. They test boundaries, adjust their actions based on system responses, and probe areas they do not fully understand. Even when using valid credentials, their interaction patterns often differ subtly from those of authorized users.

Behavioral intelligence focuses on these differences without jumping to conclusions. It recognizes that unusual behavior does not automatically indicate malicious intent. Users may change roles, systems may be updated, and workflows may evolve. What matters is whether behavior aligns with plausible explanations. Interpreting intent requires asking questions rather than making assumptions. Why is this account accessing new resources. Why has activity increased at unusual times. Why is this system being queried in unfamiliar ways. These questions guide investigation without escalating prematurely.

This focus on intent also supports proportional response. When security decisions are based solely on rule violations, responses can be blunt and disruptive. Accounts are locked, services are blocked, and operations are interrupted. Behavioral intelligence allows for more nuanced action. When intent is unclear, monitoring may be sufficient. When intent becomes more evident through continued adaptation, intervention becomes justified. This graduated approach reduces unnecessary friction while preserving security.

Understanding intent also improves collaboration. Behavioral questions often require input from multiple teams. Operations staff can explain system changes. Business units can clarify workflow shifts. Security teams can assess risk in context. This shared interpretation strengthens organizational awareness and reduces the isolation that often characterizes security functions. Behavioral intelligence thus becomes not only a technical discipline, but a communicative one.

2.3 Why Behavioral Understanding Reduces Noise and Improves Clarity

One of the most immediate challenges facing security teams is volume. Logs accumulate rapidly. Alerts fire constantly. Dashboards fill with metrics that demand attention. In such environments, meaningful signals are easily lost. Behavioral intelligence addresses this problem not by reducing data, but by improving interpretation. It introduces relevance as a guiding principle.

When behavior is understood, not every anomaly carries equal weight. Random variation is distinguished from persistent drift. Isolated events are separated from evolving patterns. This allows teams to prioritize attention where it matters most. An alert that fits into a broader narrative of change becomes more significant than an alert that appears once and never repeats. Behavioral understanding creates hierarchy within noise.

This clarity has practical consequences. Analysts spend less time chasing false positives and more time investigating meaningful patterns. Response efforts become more focused. Decision making improves because context is available. Rather than reacting to severity labels assigned by tools, teams evaluate alerts based on how they align with observed behavior. This shift reduces fatigue and increases confidence.

Behavioral understanding also improves communication beyond the security team. Technical alerts are often difficult to explain to non-specialists. Behavioral narratives are easier to convey. Describing how system usage has changed over time, or how access patterns have drifted from historical norms, provides a shared language for discussing risk. Executives and stakeholders can engage with these explanations more readily, leading to earlier involvement and better informed decisions.

Over time, this clarity contributes to stronger organizational resilience. When noise is reduced and meaning is enhanced, security becomes less reactive and more deliberate. Behavioral intelligence does not eliminate uncertainty, but it makes uncertainty manageable. It equips organizations with the ability to recognize when something is changing and to respond thoughtfully rather than urgently.

CHAPTER 3

From Logs to Meaning: Making Sense of Fragmented Signals

Modern digital systems generate enormous amounts of data. Every login, request, transaction, configuration change, and system interaction leaves a trace. These traces are captured in logs, metrics, and audit records, often stored for compliance, troubleshooting, or forensic review. Yet despite this abundance of information, organizations continue to struggle with understanding risk early. The problem is not a lack of data. It is the absence of meaning.

Logs are records, not explanations. They tell us what happened, but rarely why it matters. A log entry captures an event at a point in time, isolated from the broader sequence in which it occurred. When security teams rely on logs alone, they are forced to interpret fragments rather than narratives. Behavioral intelligence begins when logs end. It transforms fragmented signals into coherent understanding by connecting events across time, systems, and context.

One of the reasons logs feel overwhelming is that they are designed for machines, not for interpretation. They prioritize precision over perspective. A log entry may include timestamps, identifiers, and status codes, but it does not describe intention or significance. Thousands of such entries may be technically accurate and yet collectively unhelpful. Without correlation, logs become noise. Behavioral intelligence treats logs as raw material, not as finished insight.

Fragmentation is a defining characteristic of modern environments. Activity is distributed across endpoints, cloud platforms, third party services, application layers, and network infrastructure. Each component produces its own view of reality. Authentication systems record access attempts. Applications log usage. Network devices track traffic. Security tools generate alerts. Rarely are these views unified. Risk emerges in the spaces between them.

Consider how an attacker might move through such an environment. An initial login attempt appears in an authentication log. Subsequent resource access appears in application logs. Lateral movement appears in network records. None of these events, viewed independently, may raise concern. When correlated, they form a progression. Behavioral intelligence depends on this correlation. It asks how events relate, not whether they occurred.

Time plays a critical role in this process. Many security systems prioritize real time detection. While speed is valuable, it can obscure slow moving threats. Behavioral patterns often develop over extended periods. An action that occurs once may be harmless. The same action repeated weekly, with slight variation, may indicate probing. Logs preserve time, but interpretation often ignores it. Behavioral intelligence restores time as a central dimension of analysis.

Another challenge lies in volume. Large organizations generate millions of log entries daily. Analysts cannot review this data manually. Automation is necessary, but automation alone is insufficient. Filtering reduces volume, but it can also remove context. Behavioral intelligence requires selective aggregation rather than blind reduction. It seeks to group related events and examine their collective behavior.

This is where correlation becomes essential. Correlation is not simply matching identical events. It is identifying relationships between different types of activity. A login event correlates with subsequent resource access. A configuration change correlates with altered system behavior. An increase in outbound traffic correlates with unusual access patterns. These relationships create meaning. Without them, events remain isolated facts.

Correlation also demands understanding of normal behavior. Without a sense of what is typical, deviation cannot be recognized. Behavioral baselines provide reference points. These baselines are not fixed profiles. They evolve as systems and users change. Effective behavioral intelligence maintains memory without rigidity. It allows for growth while still recognizing unexplained drift.

Artificial intelligence and analytics tools can assist in this task by identifying correlations that are difficult to see manually. They can group events, detect anomalies, and highlight patterns across datasets. However, tools do not create meaning on their own. They surface possibilities. Interpretation remains a human responsibility. Behavioral intelligence depends on analysts who can ask why a correlation matters and what it suggests about intent.

A common mistake is to treat correlation as confirmation. Just because events are related does not mean they are malicious. Behavioral intelligence requires caution. It emphasizes investigation over assumption. Correlation identifies candidates for attention, not conclusions. This discipline prevents overreaction while still enabling early awareness.

Fragmented signals are also shaped by organizational structure. Different teams own different logs. Access to data may be restricted. Knowledge is siloed. Behavioral intelligence challenges this fragmentation by encouraging shared visibility. When security, operations, and development teams collaborate, context improves. Explanations emerge more quickly. Legitimate change is identified, and unexplained behavior stands out.

The transition from logs to meaning is therefore both technical and cultural. It requires systems that can collect and correlate data across boundaries. It also requires organizations willing to interpret that data collaboratively. Behavioral intelligence thrives where curiosity is valued and questioning is encouraged.

3.1 Why Event Correlation Matters More Than Individual Accuracy

In many security environments, great emphasis is placed on the accuracy of individual events. Logs are expected to be precise, timestamps synchronized, and records complete. While accuracy is important, it does not guarantee understanding. An environment can have perfectly accurate logs and still fail to recognize risk early. This happens because accuracy without connection produces fragments, not insight. Behavioral intelligence prioritizes correlation because meaning emerges from relationships, not isolated facts.

Individual events rarely explain themselves. A successful login tells us that access was granted, but it does not tell us whether the access aligns with historical behavior. A configuration change confirms that a setting was altered, but it does not explain why the change occurred at that moment or how it affects downstream systems. Behavioral intelligence treats these events as components of a larger sequence. It asks how they relate to what came before and what followed after.

Correlation allows security teams to detect patterns that would otherwise remain invisible. When authentication logs, application usage records, and network traffic data are examined together, they reveal narratives rather than snapshots. A login followed by unfamiliar resource access and then by increased outbound communication carries more significance than any of those actions alone. Behavioral intelligence depends on this layered understanding.

Focusing too narrowly on individual accuracy can also mislead teams into overconfidence. When each log entry appears legitimate, risk is assumed to be low. Correlation disrupts this assumption by showing how legitimacy can be misused. Attackers often rely on valid actions executed in unusual sequences. Behavioral intelligence exposes this misuse by emphasizing flow rather than form.

This approach also improves prioritization. In high volume environments, not every accurate event deserves equal attention. Correlation helps identify which events belong to emerging patterns and which are truly isolated. This reduces cognitive load on analysts and allows resources to be directed toward areas where behavior suggests progression rather than randomness. Over time, teams become more effective not because they see more data, but because they understand it better.

3.2 The Challenge of Fragmented Ownership and How It Obscures Meaning

One of the least discussed obstacles to behavioral intelligence is fragmented ownership of data. In many organizations, different teams control different parts of the system. Authentication logs may belong to identity teams. Application logs may sit with developers. Network data may be owned by infrastructure teams. Security teams often have partial visibility but limited authority to unify these perspectives. This fragmentation makes correlation difficult and interpretation incomplete.

When ownership is fragmented, explanations are also fragmented. A security analyst may notice unusual access behavior but lack insight into recent system changes. An operations team may observe performance anomalies without awareness of concurrent access shifts. Each team sees a portion of the picture and assumes the rest is normal. Behavioral intelligence requires these perspectives to converge.

Fragmentation also affects response. When no single team owns the full narrative, responsibility for interpretation is diluted. Signals are passed along or dismissed rather than examined collectively. Behavioral intelligence challenges this structure by insisting that meaning is shared, not siloed. Risk emerges at the boundaries between systems and teams, not within isolated domains.

Overcoming this challenge does not necessarily require reorganizing the organization. It requires creating channels for shared interpretation. Regular cross team reviews of behavioral trends. Shared baselines for critical systems. Clear mechanisms for questioning unexplained change. Behavioral intelligence thrives in environments were asking why is encouraged across roles.

When ownership remains fragmented, logs remain fragments. When ownership becomes collaborative, behavior becomes intelligible. This shift is essential for transforming security from a collection of records into a system of understanding.

CHAPTER 4

How Attackers Probe, Learn, and Adapt Over Time

Cyber-attacks are often imagined as deliberate strikes executed with precision from the outset. This image suggests that attackers arrive fully prepared, armed with complete knowledge of their targets. In reality, most attackers begin with uncertainty. They do not know the structure of a system, the behavior of its users, or the effectiveness of its controls. What they possess instead is patience. They probe, observe, learn, and adapt over time. Understanding this process is essential to recognizing threats early, because attacker behavior evolves long before an attack becomes visible.

Probing is the first stage of this process. It is exploratory rather than destructive. Attackers test how systems respond to small actions. They submit incorrect credentials to see how authentication reacts. They request resources they suspect may exist. They introduce slight variations in behavior to observe which actions trigger alerts and which pass unnoticed. Probing is designed to gather feedback. Each response from the system teaches the attacker something about boundaries, assumptions, and oversight.

This stage is rarely dramatic. Probing activity is often spread across time to avoid detection. Attempts are paced to resemble normal error rates. Requests are structured to look like legitimate use. Because probing rarely violates explicit rules, it is commonly dismissed as noise. Behavioral intelligence treats probing differently. It recognizes that probing is purposeful behavior aimed at learning, not at immediate access.

As probing continues, attackers begin to form hypotheses about the environment. They infer which accounts have elevated privileges, which systems are poorly monitored, and which interactions are trusted. This learning phase is critical. Attackers adapt their behavior based on what they observe. If a certain action triggers an alert, they avoid it. If another action passes quietly, they repeat it. Over time, their behavior becomes increasingly aligned with system expectations, making detection more difficult.

Adaptation is the defining feature of skilled attackers. They do not follow static scripts. They adjust tactics in response to resistance. When authentication controls are strong, they shift toward social engineering. When network monitoring is strict, they exploit application logic. When user behavior is closely watched, they compromise service accounts. Each adaptation is informed by prior observation. Behavioral intelligence focuses on recognizing this adaptive process rather than waiting for its outcome.

One of the most important implications of this learning cycle is that attacker behavior changes as confidence increases. Early actions are cautious and exploratory. Later actions become more deliberate and expansive. Access scopes widen. Activity frequency increases. Movement becomes more purposeful. These changes often occur gradually, blending into normal operational variation. Behavioral intelligence looks for this progression. It asks whether behavior is becoming more assertive over time and whether that assertiveness aligns with legitimate need.

Attackers also learn from human behavior. They observe how users respond to prompts, how quickly issues are reported, and which mistakes are common. Phishing campaigns are refined based on response rates. Credential reuse is exploited where policies are weak. Attackers adapt not only to systems, but to people. Behavioral intelligence therefore extends beyond technical signals to include user interaction patterns.

This adaptive process challenges traditional detection methods. Signature based systems are designed to recognize known patterns. Rule based systems enforce predefined limits. Both assume a relatively static threat model. Adaptive attackers undermine these assumptions by changing behavior before detection thresholds are crossed. Behavioral intelligence counters this by focusing on change itself rather than on specific actions.

Another aspect of attacker learning is patience. Many successful breaches unfold over months. Attackers may maintain low level access while monitoring internal processes and waiting for opportunities. They may time their actions to coincide with organizational change, staff turnover, or system upgrades. During these periods, behavioral noise increases, providing cover. Behavioral intelligence is particularly valuable here, because it can distinguish organic change from opportunistic exploitation.

Understanding attacker adaptation also changes how defense is measured. Security effectiveness is often evaluated by the absence of incidents. Behavioral intelligence suggests a different metric. How early was change recognized. How quickly was learning disrupted. How often were probing behaviors identified and questioned. These measures focus on process rather than outcome.

Defenders who understand attacker adaptation can also influence it. When probing behavior is noticed and addressed early, attackers receive feedback that their actions are visible. This may discourage continued effort or force them to abandon a path. Behavioral intelligence thus has a deterrent effect. It reduces the time attackers have to learn and adapt.

From an organizational perspective, recognizing this process requires humility. It requires acknowledging that systems are being observed just as they observe others. It requires moving beyond the idea that security controls alone are sufficient. Behavioral intelligence complements controls by focusing on how those controls are interacted with over time.

Case Study One: Slow Reconnaissance Within a Cloud Based Enterprise Environment

A mid-sized enterprise operating a hybrid cloud environment began migrating several internal applications to a public cloud platform. The migration was phased and carefully planned, involving development teams, infrastructure engineers, and security personnel. Access controls were reviewed, identity federation was enabled, and monitoring tools were deployed. From a surface perspective, the environment appeared well governed.

Several weeks after the migration began, security logs showed minor irregularities in how a small set of user accounts interacted with the new cloud resources. Access attempts occurred slightly outside normal working hours and were spread across multiple days. No account exceeded access limits. No permissions were violated. Because the organization was still adjusting to new workflows, these changes were attributed to staff adapting to the new environment.

Unbeknown to the organization, an attacker had obtained credentials through a compromised third party SaaS integration used during the migration. Rather than attempting immediate exploitation, the attacker used the access sparingly. They navigated the cloud console cautiously, viewing configurations, listing resources, and attempting low impact actions to understand how permissions were enforced. Each action was followed by a pause, allowing them to observe whether alerts were triggered or accounts were flagged.

Over time, the attacker refined their behavior. They learned which resources were monitored closely and which were not. They noticed that certain read only actions generated no alerts and that access to specific storage services was rarely reviewed. Gradually, access expanded to include data snapshots and configuration files. Still, no policy violations occurred. Every action remained within granted permissions.

The turning point came several months later, when the attacker began modifying automation scripts used by the infrastructure team. These scripts were trusted and ran with elevated privileges. By making subtle changes, the attacker gained indirect control over provisioning processes. The first visible impact was a configuration error that caused a temporary service outage.

The post incident investigation revealed a long trail of probing and learning. Authentication records showed exploratory access patterns. Resource listings increased slowly over time. Automation scripts were accessed more frequently than before. None of these actions were malicious in isolation. Together, they formed a clear progression of attacker adaptation.

The organization recognized that its failure was not technical weakness, but interpretive blindness. The attacker had learned the environment faster than the defenders had learned the attacker. After the incident, the organization introduced behavioral baselining for cloud resource access and script usage. Rather than focusing solely on violations, analysts were trained to look for gradual expansion of activity. This shift reduced future reconnaissance windows and improved early detection.

Case Study Two: Adaptive Intrusion Through Trusted Network Segments

A national infrastructure provider managed a large network supporting operational technology systems and administrative services. The environment was segmented, with strict controls between critical systems and corporate networks. Security teams focused heavily on perimeter defense and intrusion detection, confident that internal segmentation would limit damage even if access was gained.

Initial access occurred through a compromised contractor laptop that connected intermittently to the corporate network. The attacker did not attempt to move laterally immediately. Instead, they monitored network behavior. They observed which internal systems communicated regularly and which segments experienced minimal monitoring. They also learned which authentication failures triggered alerts and which did not.

The attacker began interacting with internal file shares and directory services in ways that mirrored legitimate administrative tasks. Access attempts were timed to coincide with routine maintenance windows, when network activity was higher. Requests were spaced out and varied slightly to avoid repetition. Over several weeks, the attacker built a mental map of trust relationships within the network.

As confidence grew, the attacker adapted their strategy. They identified a legacy monitoring system that bridged two network segments for reporting purposes. The system used outdated authentication methods but was considered low risk because it did not directly control critical assets. By exploiting this system, the attacker gained visibility into traffic patterns between segments.

Using this insight, the attacker slowly increased interaction with systems closer to operational technology assets. They did not breach controls directly. Instead, they leveraged existing reporting and management functions to observe system behavior. The attack remained undetected because no single action violated policy.

The intrusion was eventually discovered during an unrelated audit that reviewed changes in network communication patterns over several months. Analysts noticed that certain internal systems were exchanging data more frequently than historical baselines suggested. Further investigation revealed the compromised reporting system and the adaptive intrusion path.

The case demonstrated how attacker learning and adaptation can bypass even well designed segmentation when behavior is not interpreted holistically. The organization responded by enhancing behavioral monitoring across internal network segments. Rather than assuming trust within segments, they began tracking how trust relationships were used over time.

CHAPTER 5

The Limits of Reactive Security Models

For decades, cybersecurity has been built around reaction. An alert fires, an incident is declared, and a response is executed. This model has shaped tools, teams, metrics, and expectations across industries. It assumes that threats are best handled at the moment they become visible and that speed of response is the primary measure of effectiveness. While this approach has value, it carries significant limitations. As threats grow more adaptive and environments more complex, reactive security models increasingly reveal their shortcomings.

Reactive security is anchored in the idea of violation. Something must cross a defined boundary before attention is warranted. A rule is broken. A threshold is exceeded. A signature is matched. This framing works well for known threats and clear misuse, but it struggles with subtlety. Modern attackers rarely rush toward violation. They move cautiously, shaping their behavior to remain within accepted limits for as long as possible. By the time a reactive system responds, the attacker may already have achieved strategic positioning.

One of the central weaknesses of reactive models is their dependence on visibility at the point of impact. Alerts are designed to capture events that are already problematic. They are less effective at recognizing conditions that are becoming risky. This creates a narrow window for prevention. Security teams are forced to operate under urgency, often making decisions with incomplete context. The result is containment rather than understanding.

Reactive models also encourage a fragmented view of risk. Because alerts are generated by individual systems, each event is treated independently. An authentication alert is examined separately from a network anomaly. An application error is reviewed without reference to recent access changes. This separation reinforces event based thinking and obscures patterns that span systems and time. Behavioral intelligence highlights this fragmentation as a structural flaw rather than an operational oversight.

Another limitation lies in how success is measured. Reactive security emphasizes metrics such as time to detect and time to respond. While these metrics are useful, they implicitly accept that detection will occur late. They reward efficiency after compromise rather than awareness before it. Over time, organizations may become highly skilled at managing incidents without becoming better at preventing them. This creates a false sense of maturity.

Alert fatigue is a predictable outcome of reactive models. As environments scale, the number of events that meet alerting criteria increases. Security teams are flooded with notifications, many of which lack clear relevance. Analysts are forced to triage constantly, suppressing noise to preserve capacity. In this environment, early signals that do not trigger alerts are easily ignored. Behavioral intelligence recognizes alert fatigue not as a human failure, but as a design failure.

Reactive models also struggle with adaptation. Attackers learn how systems respond and adjust their behavior accordingly. When an alert is triggered, attackers change tactics. When a control blocks an action, they find an alternative path. Reactive systems respond to yesterday's behavior. Attackers prepare for tomorrow's response. This imbalance favors those who adapt faster.

The reliance on predefined rules further limits reactive security. Rules are based on assumptions about how threats behave. As threats evolve, rules must be updated. This creates a constant race between defenders and attackers. Behavioral intelligence shifts the focus from rules to observation. It does not attempt to predict every possible attack. It focuses on detecting when behavior changes in ways that suggest learning or intent.

Reactive security models also influence organizational culture. Teams become oriented around firefighting. Success is defined by how quickly incidents are closed rather than how often they are avoided. Learning tends to occur after failure, during post incident reviews, rather than continuously. Behavioral intelligence encourages a different culture. It values curiosity, pattern recognition, and early questioning. It treats near misses as opportunities for insight rather than inconveniences.

From a strategic perspective, reactive security limits leadership understanding. Executives are often informed of incidents after damage has occurred. Decisions are made under pressure. Long term patterns are obscured by short term urgency. Behavioral intelligence provides a way to communicate risk earlier and more clearly. It allows leaders to see change developing rather than reacting to disruption.

Reactive models also struggle in environments where trust is abused rather than broken. Credential based attacks, insider misuse, and supply chain compromise often involve legitimate actions executed with malicious intent. Reactive systems assume that legitimacy equals safety. Behavioral intelligence challenges this assumption by examining how legitimate actions are used over time. It recognizes that trust relationships can be exploited gradually.

The limits of reactive security do not mean it should be abandoned. Response capabilities remain essential. Incidents will occur, and organizations must be able to contain them. The problem arises when reaction becomes the primary strategy rather than a component of a broader approach. Behavioral intelligence complements reactive security by extending the timeline of defense. It brings attention to the period before alerts fire.

As digital systems become more interconnected, the cost of delayed understanding increases. A breach in one system can cascade across others. Service disruptions can affect millions. Trust can erode quickly. Reactive security responds after the fact. Behavioral intelligence seeks to prevent escalation by recognizing change early.

5.1 Why Speed Without Insight Often Leads to Repeated Failure

Speed has become one of the most celebrated indicators of cybersecurity competence. Organizations proudly measure how quickly incidents are detected, how fast systems are isolated, and how rapidly services are restored. These metrics create the impression of control and readiness. However, when speed becomes the primary objective, it often conceals a deeper weakness. Rapid response without insight tends to address symptoms repeatedly while leaving underlying conditions unchanged.

In environments driven by urgency, security teams are trained to act immediately once an alert is raised. Playbooks are followed, containment steps are executed, and normal operations are restored as quickly as possible. While this approach limits immediate damage, it rarely creates space for understanding how the situation developed in the first place. Behavioral signals that appeared days or weeks earlier are overshadowed by the pressure to resolve the visible problem. Once the incident is closed, attention shifts elsewhere.

This pattern leads to recurrence. Similar incidents resurface because the behavioral conditions that allowed them to form were never examined. Attackers recognize this weakness. They learn that organizations are effective at response but slow at interpretation. As a result, they adapt their behavior to exploit the same blind spots repeatedly, knowing that defenders will react only when thresholds are crossed.

Speed driven models also distort prioritization. When everything is urgent, nothing is fully understood. Analysts focus on clearing queues rather than building narratives. Alerts are resolved individually rather than connected. Over time, security operations become transactional. Success is defined by closure rates rather than by reduction in uncertainty. Behavioral intelligence exposes this limitation by shifting attention from how fast something is fixed to how early it is understood.

Another consequence of speed without insight is exhaustion. Constant urgency erodes analytical capacity. Teams operating under perpetual pressure have little opportunity to step back and observe trends. Fatigue sets in, and attention narrows to the most obvious issues. Subtle behavioral changes that do not demand immediate action are easily overlooked. Ironically, the pursuit of speed makes organizations slower to recognize emerging risk.

Behavioral intelligence offers an alternative timeline. Instead of waiting for urgency, it encourages early curiosity. It asks teams to notice gradual change and ask questions before response becomes necessary. When insight precedes action, intervention becomes deliberate rather than reactive. Incidents are disrupted during formation rather than managed after consolidation. In this sense, insight does not slow security down. It reduces the need for speed by preventing crisis altogether.

5.2 The Hidden Cost of Treating Security as a Series of Incidents

Another structural weakness of reactive security models is the way they frame risk as a sequence of isolated incidents. Each breach, intrusion, or disruption is treated as a self-contained event with its own cause and resolution. Reports are written, lessons are documented, and the organization moves forward. What this approach misses is continuity. Behavioral intelligence reveals that many incidents are connected through shared behavioral patterns that unfold over long periods.

When security is organized around incidents, long term observation is devalued. Low level anomalies that persist across months are dismissed because they never trigger escalation. Minor access irregularities are overlooked because they resolve themselves. Gradual expansion of system usage is accepted as organic growth. Each occurrence is too small to justify concern on its own. Behavioral intelligence shows how these fragments accumulate into systemic exposure.

This incident centric mindset also weakens organizational memory. Knowledge is captured in post incident reports rather than embedded in practice. Teams remember what failed, but not how behavior changed leading up to failure. As personnel rotate and priorities shift, these lessons fade. The same patterns reappear, and the organization is surprised by familiar problems. Behavioral intelligence insists that memory must be continuous, not episodic.

There is also a strategic cost. Leaders who receive information only after incidents occur are forced into reactive decision making. Investments are driven by the most recent failure rather than by observed trends. Resources are allocated to address yesterday's problem rather than tomorrow's risk.

Behavioral intelligence provides a broader view. It allows leadership to see how risk is evolving across systems and time, enabling more informed planning.

Treating security as a series of incidents also shapes culture. Teams become accustomed to firefighting. Recognition is tied to crisis response rather than to quiet prevention. Over time, this discourages careful observation and rewards urgency. Behavioral intelligence challenges this culture by valuing attention, patience, and interpretation. It reframes security as an ongoing practice rather than a collection of emergencies.

The hidden cost of incident focused security is not always measured in breaches alone. It appears as repeated disruption, declining confidence, and increasing effort required to maintain stability. Organizations may invest heavily in tools and staff while still experiencing familiar failures. Behavioral intelligence reveals that the missing element is not capability, but continuity.

By shifting focus from isolated incidents to behavioral patterns, organizations gain a clearer understanding of how risk develops and persists. Security becomes less about reacting to what has already happened and more about recognizing what is taking shape. This shift does not eliminate incidents entirely, but it reduces their frequency and severity by addressing the conditions that allow them to emerge.

CHAPTER 6

Applying Artificial Intelligence Without Losing Context

Artificial intelligence has become a central feature of modern cybersecurity. Machine learning models classify behavior, analytics engines surface anomalies, and automated systems promise faster detection and response. In many organizations, AI is viewed as a solution to scale, a way to manage data volumes that exceed human capacity. While these technologies offer genuine value, they also introduce a significant risk. When artificial intelligence is applied without context, it can obscure understanding rather than enhance it.

The core challenge lies in how intelligence is defined. Artificial intelligence excels at recognizing patterns, but pattern recognition alone does not equal understanding. A model can identify deviation from a baseline, but it cannot determine why that deviation matters unless it is designed with behavioral context in mind. Without this context, AI systems may flag activity that is unusual but harmless, while missing activity that is subtle but meaningful. Behavioral intelligence provides the framework that allows artificial intelligence to function as an aid rather than a replacement for judgment.

One of the most common mistakes in applying AI to security is treating automation as an end rather than a means. Organizations deploy models to reduce analyst workload, suppress noise, and accelerate response. While these goals are reasonable, they can lead to over reliance on outputs that are not fully understood. Alerts generated by algorithms are often accepted or dismissed without interrogation. Over time, this erodes analytical thinking. Behavioral intelligence insists that AI outputs be questioned, interpreted, and validated within the broader narrative of system behavior.

Context begins with understanding normal behavior. Machine learning models are trained on historical data to establish baselines. However, history does not always represent intent. Past behavior may include undetected misuse, policy drift, or temporary anomalies. When models learn from such data without critical review, they inherit its blind spots. Behavioral intelligence demands that baselines be examined, not just calculated. It requires human input to distinguish between stable behavior and tolerated risk.

Another challenge arises from the dynamic nature of digital environments. Systems change, users adapt, and workloads fluctuate. Models trained on static snapshots struggle to keep pace. They may generate false positives during legitimate change or fail to recognize slow moving threats that adapt gradually. Behavioral intelligence addresses this by emphasizing evolution rather than fixed thresholds. Artificial intelligence must be designed to learn continuously while preserving memory of meaningful change. This balance is difficult but necessary.

Interpretability is also crucial. Many advanced models operate as black boxes, producing scores or classifications without explanation. While these outputs may be statistically sound, they offer little guidance for action. Analysts are left to trust or ignore results without understanding their basis. Behavioral intelligence prioritizes explainability. It values models that can show which behaviors contributed to a decision and how those behaviors relate over time. This transparency supports learning and accountability.

Artificial intelligence is most effective when it augments human capability rather than replacing it. Humans excel at contextual reasoning, intuition, and hypothesis formation. Machines excel at processing volume and detecting correlation. Behavioral intelligence integrates these strengths. AI surfaces patterns that warrant attention. Humans interpret those patterns within organizational, operational, and historical context. This partnership reduces noise while preserving meaning.

The role of artificial intelligence also extends beyond detection. It can support behavioral analysis by identifying trends, grouping related events, and highlighting sequences that span systems. It can assist in prioritization by ranking behavioral drift based on persistence and scope. However, it should not be used to automate judgment. Decisions about risk, response, and escalation require understanding that models alone cannot provide.

There is also an organizational dimension to consider. When AI is introduced without clarity, teams may defer responsibility to technology. Alerts are trusted because they are generated by algorithms. Silence is interpreted as safety. Behavioral intelligence challenges this complacency. It reminds organizations that absence of alerts does not equal absence of risk. AI systems are tools, not authorities. They reflect the assumptions and limitations embedded within them.

From a strategic perspective, applying artificial intelligence without losing context requires deliberate design choices. Models should be aligned with behavioral questions rather than generic anomaly detection. Training data should be reviewed for bias and blind spots. Outputs should be interpretable and integrated into workflows that encourage inquiry. Analysts should be trained to use AI as a lens, not as a verdict.

6.1 When Automation Replaces Curiosity

One of the most overlooked risks in adopting artificial intelligence for cybersecurity is not technical failure, but behavioral complacency. As organizations introduce machine learning models and automated decision engines into their security operations, there is a subtle shift in how analysts engage with their environment. Curiosity, which is essential to behavioral intelligence, can slowly give way to reliance. Instead of asking why something is happening, teams begin to ask only whether the system has flagged it. Over time, this shift narrows perception and weakens defensive awareness.

Automation is often introduced to manage scale. Faced with overwhelming volumes of data, organizations seek relief through tools that promise prioritization and clarity. However, when automation becomes the primary filter through which activity is interpreted, it can unintentionally suppress early behavioral signals. Models are trained to identify patterns that match predefined notions of risk. Behavior that falls outside those notions may be ignored, not because it is harmless, but because it is unfamiliar.

This creates a dangerous feedback loop. Analysts trust automated outputs because they appear objective. Silence from the system is interpreted as safety. Over time, teams lose confidence in their own observation. They stop tracking subtle change unless it is validated by a model. Behavioral intelligence is undermined not by the presence of AI, but by the absence of questioning around it.

The problem is compounded when organizations treat automation as an authority rather than a tool. Alerts generated by models are escalated quickly, sometimes without sufficient context. Meanwhile, areas not covered by models receive little attention. This selective visibility creates blind spots. Attackers who understand the boundaries of automated detection learn to operate just outside them, adapting behavior to remain below the threshold of algorithmic concern.

Behavioral intelligence insists that automation should provoke questions, not answer them definitively. A model that highlights unusual behavior should prompt analysts to ask what that behavior represents within the broader system narrative. Equally, the absence of alerts should not end inquiry. It should invite periodic review of whether assumptions remain valid. Automation should widen perspective, not narrow it.

This balance requires organizational discipline. Analysts must be encouraged to challenge automated conclusions. Time must be allocated for exploratory analysis rather than constant alert handling. Leadership must value insight as much as efficiency. Without these supports, artificial intelligence risks accelerating ignorance rather than reducing it.

Case Study: Automated Silence in a Financial Technology Platform

A rapidly growing financial technology company implemented an advanced machine learning based security monitoring platform to manage increasing transaction volumes and user activity. The platform used behavioral analytics to flag anomalies across authentication, transaction processing, and account access. Early results were encouraging. Alert volumes decreased significantly, and response times improved. The security team gained confidence in the system and gradually reduced manual review of activity streams.

Several months later, a small number of user accounts began exhibiting subtle behavioral changes. Transaction frequency increased slightly, but remained within normal ranges. Access patterns shifted toward less commonly used features. The timing of activity drifted toward early morning hours. None of these changes were flagged by the automated system because they did not deviate sharply enough from learned baselines.

Unbeknown to the organization, attackers had compromised a set of accounts through credential reuse. They deliberately limited their activity to remain below detection thresholds. Over time, they tested transaction limits, observed response delays, and identified opportunities for abuse. The automated system remained silent. Analysts assumed the absence of alerts indicated stability.

The incident came to light only when customer complaints revealed unauthorized withdrawals. Investigation showed that behavioral changes had been present for weeks. The data existed, but it was never examined because it was not highlighted by the model. Analysts had trusted automation to surface risk and had stopped asking what might be forming beneath the surface.

In response, the organization restructured its approach. Automation remained in place, but analysts were tasked with periodic behavioral reviews independent of alerts. Models were adjusted to surface gradual drift rather than sharp deviation. Most importantly, team culture changed. Analysts were encouraged to treat automated silence as a prompt for reflection rather than reassurance.

6.2 The Risk of Training Models on Compromised or Incomplete Behavior

Another critical challenge in applying artificial intelligence to cybersecurity lies in how models are trained. Machine learning systems learn from history. They absorb past behavior, identify patterns, and use those patterns to judge future activity. This process assumes that historical data accurately represents healthy system behavior. In reality, this assumption is often flawed. Many environments contain undetected misuse, tolerated risk, or long standing configuration weaknesses. When models are trained on such data, they inherit its distortions.

Behavioral intelligence warns against confusing familiarity with safety. Just because an action has occurred repeatedly in the past does not mean it is benign. In some cases, repeated behavior reflects a blind spot rather than legitimacy. When artificial intelligence models treat these patterns as normal, they reinforce them. Risk becomes invisible not because it disappears, but because it has been learned.

Incomplete data creates a similar problem. Models trained on limited visibility develop narrow perspectives. If certain systems, user groups, or time periods are underrepresented, the model's understanding of behavior is skewed. Activity outside that learned scope may be misclassified or ignored. Behavioral intelligence emphasizes that absence of data is itself a signal. Artificial intelligence systems, however, struggle to recognize what they have not seen.

This issue is particularly dangerous in environments that undergo frequent change. Mergers, rapid growth, cloud migration, and remote work all introduce new behavioral patterns. If models are trained before or during these transitions without careful oversight, they may confuse transition noise with stability. Attackers who exploit this confusion can operate under the cover of organizational change.

Behavioral intelligence therefore demands intentional training practices. Historical data must be reviewed critically. Analysts must ask whether past behavior represents best practice or merely accepted reality. Training periods should be chosen deliberately, and models should be retrained with awareness of environmental shifts. Without this discipline, artificial intelligence becomes a mirror of past mistakes rather than a tool for future resilience.

Case Study: Normalized Risk in a Large Enterprise Network

A large enterprise with a distributed workforce adopted an AI driven security analytics platform to monitor internal behavior across endpoints, applications, and network traffic. The system was trained on several years of historical data to establish behavioral baselines. At the time of deployment, leadership praised the platform for its low false positive rate and its ability to suppress routine noise.

What was not fully considered was the quality of the historical data used for training. For years, the organization had tolerated weak internal segmentation and broad administrative access. Certain service accounts were used across multiple systems with minimal oversight. These practices were well known but had never resulted in visible incidents. As a result, they were accepted as normal.

The AI model learned this behavior. Broad access patterns were classified as expected. Repeated use of service accounts across environments was treated as stable activity. When an attacker later compromised one of these service accounts through a supply chain vulnerability, their movement blended seamlessly into learned baselines. Lateral activity occurred at a scale that would have been alarming in a better segmented environment, but the model did not flag it because it resembled historical patterns.

The breach was eventually discovered through a manual investigation triggered by unrelated system instability. Analysts reviewing the timeline realized that the attacker's behavior was indistinguishable from accepted internal behavior. The model had not failed technically. It had succeeded in learning a flawed reality.

In the aftermath, the organization reassessed its approach. Historical data was segmented into trusted and questionable periods. Models were retrained using stricter definitions of acceptable behavior. Behavioral intelligence principles were introduced to guide training decisions. Analysts were encouraged to question whether learned patterns represented desired behavior rather than familiar behavior.

CHAPTER 7

From Detection to Prediction: Anticipating Threats Before Impact

Cybersecurity has traditionally been structured around detection. Systems are designed to identify threats once they become visible through alerts, violations, or failures. This approach assumes that risk becomes actionable only after it crosses a defined boundary. While detection remains necessary, it places defenders in a position of response rather than control. Prediction seeks to change that posture by identifying conditions that make compromise likely before damage occurs.

Prediction in cybersecurity does not involve forecasting specific attacks or identifying future adversaries. It is concerned with recognizing behavioral trajectories that historically precede security incidents. Behavioral intelligence provides the foundation for this approach by observing how activity evolves over time. Rather than asking whether a system has been breached, predictive security asks whether the environment is moving toward a state where breach becomes easier to execute and harder to contain.

A central concept in prediction is accumulation. Risk does not usually emerge from a single event. It develops through small, often tolerated changes that compound over time. Access privileges expand incrementally. Monitoring exceptions become permanent. Operational shortcuts are normalized. Behavioral intelligence tracks these accumulations and examines how they interact. Prediction becomes possible when these elements are understood as parts of a broader progression rather than as isolated adjustments.

Prediction also depends heavily on continuity of observation. Systems that reset their understanding of behavior frequently lose the ability to recognize gradual drift. Behavioral intelligence insists on maintaining memory. This memory does not freeze systems in the past, but it preserves awareness of how current behavior compares to earlier states. When defenders understand where a system started and how it has changed, they can identify when change becomes directional rather than incidental.

Another requirement for prediction is disciplined interpretation. Not every behavioral change is meaningful. Systems evolve, users adapt, and workloads fluctuate. Predictive security requires distinguishing between expected evolution and unexplained deviation. This distinction cannot be automated entirely. It relies on analysts who understand operational context and can evaluate whether behavioral change aligns with legitimate causes. Behavioral intelligence supports this judgment by providing structured visibility into how behavior shifts over time.

Prediction also alters how security teams prioritize effort. In reactive models, attention is driven by alerts and incidents. In predictive models, attention is guided by likelihood and trajectory. Systems exhibiting accelerating change receive more scrutiny than those showing stable variation. This allows teams to intervene earlier and more selectively. Resources are applied where risk is forming rather than where damage has already occurred.

Intervention in predictive security is not always disruptive. Often it involves clarification rather than containment. A role change may explain new access patterns. A system upgrade may account for increased activity. When explanations are valid, monitoring continues without escalation. When explanations are absent or inconsistent, intervention becomes justified. Behavioral intelligence enables this graduated response by framing investigation as inquiry rather than accusation.

Prediction also changes how security is discussed internally. Instead of reporting incidents after the fact, teams communicate emerging conditions. This requires a different vocabulary. Rather than stating that a system has been compromised, teams explain that access patterns are expanding in ways that historically lead to misuse. Rather than presenting alerts, they present trends. This approach supports earlier decision making and reduces the pressure associated with crisis response.

Importantly, prediction does not claim certainty. It operates in probability and confidence, not absolutes. Behavioral intelligence does not promise to eliminate breaches. It reduces their likelihood and severity by shortening the window between emergence and recognition. Prediction allows organizations to act while options remain flexible rather than when responses are constrained.

From an operational perspective, predictive security requires adjustment in tooling, workflows, and mindset. Tools must support longitudinal analysis rather than snapshot alerts. Workflows must allow time for interpretation rather than constant triage. Analysts must be trained to recognize progression rather than wait for violation. Behavioral intelligence provides the structure needed to support these changes.

Prediction is therefore not a replacement for detection, but an extension of it. Detection identifies what has happened. Prediction identifies what is becoming likely. Behavioral intelligence connects the two by revealing how behavior moves from normal variation to elevated risk. When this connection is understood, security becomes less reactive and more deliberate, focused on preventing escalation rather than managing aftermath.

7.1 Recognizing Behavioral Trajectories That Signal Escalation

Predictive security relies heavily on the ability to recognize behavioral trajectories rather than isolated deviations. A trajectory reflects how behavior changes in direction, intensity, and scope over time. Unlike static anomalies, trajectories reveal momentum. They show whether activity is stabilizing, plateauing, or progressively expanding. Behavioral intelligence treats this momentum as more meaningful than any single data point.

In practice, trajectories often emerge quietly. Access privileges may increase incrementally through role adjustments, temporary permissions that are never revoked, or repeated exceptions granted for convenience. Activity may shift gradually toward systems that were previously untouched. Frequency may rise in subtle increments that remain within acceptable thresholds. None of these actions independently justify alarm. When observed collectively and sequentially, they indicate growing capability or confidence.

Behavioral intelligence enables defenders to observe these movements longitudinally. Instead of asking whether an action violates policy, predictive analysis asks whether behavior is trending toward higher leverage within the environment. Escalation is recognized not by severity, but by direction. A user who consistently expands reach without corresponding responsibility represents a different risk profile from one whose behavior remains bounded and predictable.

This approach also reframes how uncertainty is handled. Predictive security does not require certainty to be useful. It operates on increasing confidence. As trajectories become clearer, confidence grows. Intervention timing is guided by this confidence rather than by rigid thresholds. This allows organizations to engage earlier, when explanations can still be sought and corrective action can be subtle.

Recognizing trajectories also requires resisting complacency. Gradual change is easy to normalize, especially in fast moving environments. Behavioral intelligence challenges this by preserving memory of earlier states. It reminds analysts not only of what behavior looks like now, but of how it arrived there. This temporal awareness is essential for identifying escalation before it hardens into misuse.

7.2 Separating Legitimate Evolution From Behavioral Drift

A major challenge in predictive security is determining whether observed behavioral change reflects legitimate evolution or unaddressed drift. Digital systems evolve continuously. Teams reorganize. Responsibilities shift. New tools are adopted. Behavioral intelligence does not treat change as suspicious by default. It treats unexplained change as unresolved.

Legitimate evolution is usually accompanied by context. A new project explains expanded access. A system migration explains increased activity. A role change explains altered usage patterns. Behavioral intelligence depends on this contextual alignment. When behavior changes and explanation follow naturally, risk remains low. When behavior changes without clear justification, uncertainty increases.

Predictive security formalizes this distinction. Instead of suppressing alerts or blindly accepting change, it introduces inquiry as a standard response. Analysts ask whether behavioral shifts align with documented decisions, operational plans, or organizational intent. When alignment exists, baselines are adjusted deliberately. When alignment is absent, behavior remains under observation.

This process prevents two common failures. The first is overreaction, where legitimate change is mistaken for threat. The second is neglect, where risky drift is accepted because it does not immediately cause harm. Behavioral intelligence provides a middle path. It allows systems to evolve without losing visibility into how that evolution affects exposure.

Over time, organizations that practice this discipline develop a stronger sense of behavioral identity. They understand not just what their systems do, but how they are meant to behave under different conditions. This clarity improves prediction quality and reduces dependency on rigid rules. Separation between evolution and drift becomes more accurate as institutional understanding deepens.

Importantly, this distinction also preserves trust. Users are not treated as suspects simply because their behavior changes. Instead, behavior is interpreted within a shared operational narrative. Predictive security becomes collaborative rather than adversarial, grounded in explanation rather than accusation.

7.3 Using Predictive Insight to Shape Proportionate and Timely Action

Prediction has value only when it informs action in a controlled and proportionate way. Behavioral intelligence does not advocate immediate escalation at the first sign of emerging risk. It enables graduated response based on confidence, potential impact, and available context. This approach replaces abrupt reaction with measured intervention.

Early predictive signals often warrant minimal action. Increased observation, clarification requests, or temporary constraints may be sufficient. These actions are reversible and non-disruptive. They allow organizations to gather more information without creating unnecessary friction. As behavioral confidence increases, responses can scale accordingly.

Proportionate action also reduces operational damage. Reactive security often intervenes at the most disruptive point, when systems are already compromised or misuse is evident. Predictive security intervenes earlier, when options are broader and consequences are smaller. This preserves continuity while still reducing exposure.

Behavioral intelligence supports this approach by making justification visible. Decisions are based on observable progression rather than opaque alerts. This transparency improves internal communication and accountability. Stakeholders understand why actions are taken and how risk assessments were formed.

In practice, predictive insight reshapes security workflows. Analysts move from constant alert triage to periodic behavioral review. Leaders receive information about emerging conditions rather than post incident summaries. Decisions are informed by direction and likelihood rather than by urgency alone.

This does not eliminate incidents. It reduces surprise. When incidents do occur, they are often anticipated, contained earlier, and less disruptive. Behavioral intelligence enables security teams to act while still in control of timing and scope. Prediction, applied carefully, transforms security from a defensive reaction into a managed process of risk containment.

CHAPTER 8

Ethics, Trust, and the Boundaries of Behavioral Analysis

Behavioral intelligence introduces a powerful shift in how cybersecurity risk is identified and managed. By analyzing patterns of interaction over time, organizations gain earlier visibility into emerging threats that would otherwise remain hidden. However, this proximity to user behavior introduces ethical complexity. Behavioral analysis sits close to human decision making, intent, and routine. Without clearly defined boundaries, it can move from protective oversight into invasive surveillance. This chapter examines how behavioral intelligence can be applied responsibly, preserving trust while maintaining its effectiveness as a security discipline.

At the center of ethical behavioral analysis is purpose. Behavioral intelligence must exist to protect systems, data, and operations. It should not be used to evaluate personal performance, enforce discipline, or monitor individuals beyond what is necessary for security. When purpose becomes blurred, trust erodes. Users begin to question why their behavior is being observed and how the information might be used. Ethical clarity begins by stating explicitly what behavioral intelligence is designed to do and what it is not designed to do.

Trust is not a byproduct of security. It is a prerequisite for it. Systems that rely on behavioral data depend on users interacting naturally with digital environments. When users feel watched unfairly or evaluated continuously, behavior changes. They become cautious, defensive, or evasive. This distorts data and weakens security insight. Behavioral intelligence therefore depends on an implicit contract. Observation exists to reduce risk, not to exert control. Maintaining this contract requires consistency, transparency, and restraint.

One of the most significant ethical risks in behavioral intelligence is scope expansion. Security teams often deploy behavioral tools with narrow objectives, such as detecting credential misuse or identifying anomalous access. Over time, these tools reveal additional insights that appear useful for other purposes. Productivity trends, behavioral efficiency, or compliance monitoring may become tempting applications. Each expansion alters the relationship between organization and user. Ethical practice demands that behavioral intelligence not be repurposed casually. Any expansion of scope must be deliberate, justified, and governed.

Data collection practices also define ethical boundaries. Behavioral intelligence does not benefit from excessive data. It benefits from relevant data. Collecting more information than necessary increases exposure, complicates interpretation, and raises questions about intent. Ethical programmers practice data minimization. They identify which behavioral signals are necessary for risk analysis and exclude those that are not. This discipline protects users and improves analytical quality by reducing noise.

Interpretation introduces another layer of responsibility. Behavioral signals indicate probability, not certainty. They suggest elevated risk, not wrongdoing. Treating behavioral indicators as proof leads to unfair decisions and undermines credibility. Ethical behavioral intelligence requires human oversight at every critical decision point. Automated scoring may guide attention, but it should not dictate outcomes. Analysts must interpret signals within context, seek explanation, and allow for legitimate variation.

Bias is an unavoidable concern. Behavioral models learn from historical data and operational assumptions. If past behavior includes tolerated misuse, unequal treatment, or structural imbalance, models may normalize these patterns. Ethical application requires continuous review of training data, model outputs, and decision outcomes. Analysts must be empowered to question whether a model reflects desired behavior or inherited compromise. Behavioral intelligence without oversight risks reinforcing existing weaknesses rather than correcting them.

Governance structures provide the framework that sustains ethical practice. Clear ownership ensures accountability. Policies should define who can access behavioral data, how long it is retained, and under what conditions it can be reviewed. Oversight mechanisms, such as periodic audits and cross functional review, help prevent misuse and drift. Without governance, behavioral intelligence becomes vulnerable to misinterpretation and abuse.

Communication plays a decisive role in maintaining trust. Users do not need to understand technical details, but they do need to understand intent. Organizations that explain behavioral intelligence as a protective measure rather than a monitoring tool create space for cooperation. Silence or ambiguity breeds' suspicion. Clear communication reinforces legitimacy and reduces resistance during investigations or intervention.

Ethical discipline also protects security practitioners. Analysts working without clear boundaries may be pressured to act on ambiguous signals or justify decisions without guidance. This creates personal and professional risk. Clear ethical frameworks support consistent decision making and protect practitioners from unreasonable expectations. Behavioral intelligence works best when analysts are guided by principle rather than improvisation.

Importantly, ethical application strengthens security rather than weakening it. Systems that respect boundaries produce more reliable data. Users behave naturally when they trust intent. Investigations proceed with cooperation rather than resistance. Over time, behavioral intelligence becomes a stabilizing force rather than a source of tension.

Behavioral intelligence is not just a technical capability. It is a responsibility. Its effectiveness depends on how carefully it is governed and how deliberately it is applied. Security that compromises trust eventually undermines itself. Behavioral intelligence must therefore be practiced with restraint, clarity, and respect for the boundaries that make sustained protection possible.

8.1 Balancing Behavioral Visibility With User Autonomy

One of the most delicate challenges in behavioral intelligence is determining how much visibility is enough. Security teams require sufficient behavioral insight to recognize emerging risk, yet excessive visibility can undermine user autonomy and distort behavior itself. When users feel overly scrutinized, they may alter how they interact with systems in ways that reduce both productivity and analytical accuracy. Behavioral intelligence must therefore strike a balance between observation and restraint.

Autonomy matters because behavioral intelligence depends on natural behavior. The value of behavioral signals lies in their authenticity. If users begin to act defensively or artificially to avoid scrutiny, the data becomes less representative. Patterns flatten. Variability disappears. Analysts lose the subtle signals that indicate genuine change. Ethical behavioral intelligence protects autonomy by limiting observation to behaviors that are directly relevant to system security and risk formation.

This balance is achieved through intentional design. Behavioral monitoring should focus on interaction patterns rather than content wherever possible. It should emphasize how systems are accessed, not what individuals are working on. By abstracting behavior to structural signals, frequency, scope, sequence, timing, organizations reduce intrusion while preserving insight. Behavioral intelligence is most effective when it observes structure rather than intention.

Clear boundaries also support autonomy. Users should not feel that every action is being evaluated continuously. Instead, behavioral intelligence should operate quietly, surfacing patterns only when change becomes sustained or directional. This reduces unnecessary attention and preserves trust. Analysts engage only when behavior warrants interpretation, not as a routine response to normal variation.

Autonomy is further supported by proportional response. When behavioral signals prompt inquiry, the initial interaction should be explanatory rather than corrective. Seeking clarification respects agency and often resolves uncertainty without escalation. Behavioral intelligence should invite dialogue before enforcement. This approach preserves dignity while still protecting systems.

Over time, organizations that respect autonomy benefit from higher quality behavioral data. Users interact freely, systems reflect genuine usage, and analysts gain clearer insight into how environments actually function. Behavioral intelligence becomes a background discipline rather than a visible constraint.

Case Study: Behavioral Monitoring in a Distributed Workforce Environment

A technology services company with a large remote workforce introduced behavioral intelligence to address increasing credential misuse and access anomalies. The initial deployment focused heavily on user activity monitoring, including detailed tracking of session duration, application usage, and interaction timing. While the system generated rich data, it also triggered concern among employees, many of whom felt that productivity rather than security was being measured.

Within months, security analysts noticed a change in behavior. Users began consolidating tasks to reduce perceived exposure. Access patterns became rigid and predictable. Variability dropped sharply. While this initially appeared positive, analysts realized that the behavioral data no longer reflected natural workflows. The system had achieved visibility at the cost of authenticity.

Following internal review, the organization revised its approach. Behavioral intelligence was refocused on security relevant signals such as access scope expansion, unusual sequencing of actions, and cross system correlation. Content level monitoring was removed. Communication was improved to clarify purpose and boundaries. Users were informed that behavioral analysis existed to protect access and systems, not to assess performance.

Over time, behavior normalized. Variability returned. Analysts regained the ability to detect subtle drift and emerging risk. Incidents of credential misuse declined as early signals became clearer. The organization concluded that behavioral intelligence is most effective when users are aware of its presence but confident in its limits.

8.2 Establishing Accountability Without Creating a Culture of Suspicion

Another ethical boundary in behavioral intelligence lies in how accountability is enforced. Security programmers must be able to act on behavioral signals, yet doing so without care can foster a culture of suspicion. When behavioral analysis is perceived as a mechanism for blame rather than protection, cooperation deteriorates. Users become guarded, explanations are withheld, and legitimate anomalies are concealed rather than clarified. Behavioral intelligence loses effectiveness when trust is replaced by fear.

Accountability in this context should not mean constant scrutiny of individuals. It should mean clarity of responsibility for systems, access paths, and decisions. Behavioral intelligence works best when it highlights conditions and patterns rather than pointing to people prematurely. Signals should indicate where behavior has changed, not who is at fault. Investigation should focus on understanding how risk emerged, not assigning blame for its presence.

This distinction affects how alerts and findings are communicated internally. When behavioral insights are framed as questions rather than conclusions, dialogue becomes possible. Analysts can ask why a certain access path expanded or why activity shifted without implying misconduct. This approach preserves psychological safety while still enabling corrective action. Accountability is maintained through explanation and adjustment rather than accusation.

Leadership behavior plays a critical role here. When executives treat behavioral intelligence as a governance tool rather than a disciplinary one, tone cascades through the organization. Teams become more willing to report uncertainty, document exceptions, and explain deviations. Behavioral intelligence becomes a shared responsibility rather than a surveillance mechanism. Without this tone, even well designed systems can be misused.

Formal processes also help maintain balance. Clear escalation paths, documentation standards, and review mechanisms ensure that behavioral findings are handled consistently. Decisions are recorded, reasoning is visible, and outcomes are reviewed. This reduces arbitrary enforcement and protects both users and analysts. Behavioral intelligence requires process maturity as much as technical capability.

Over time, organizations that establish accountability without suspicion develop stronger behavioral baselines. Users feel safe to operate normally and to explain changes when they occur. Analysts receive better context and can distinguish risk from evolution more accurately. Behavioral intelligence becomes a tool for alignment rather than enforcement.

Case Study: Behavioral Intelligence in a Regulated Financial Services Organization

A regulated financial services organization introduced behavioral intelligence to strengthen oversight of privileged access. Early implementation focused on tracking administrator behavior across critical systems. While technically effective, the programme quickly encountered resistance. Administrators felt targeted and assumed that the system existed to identify mistakes or misconduct. Informal workarounds emerged, and explanations for unusual behavior became less forthcoming.

Security leaders recognized that the issue was not the technology but the framing. Behavioral intelligence had been introduced without clear accountability principles. Findings were escalated directly to management without prior discussion, creating an adversarial dynamic. Behavioral signals were treated as evidence rather than indicators.

The organization revised its approach. Behavioral findings were first reviewed collaboratively between security and system owners. Signals prompted joint analysis rather than immediate reporting. Only unresolved or high confidence risks were escalated formally. Documentation emphasized system conditions rather than individual actions.

Within months, cooperation improved. Administrators began proactively explaining access changes and documenting temporary exceptions. Behavioral baselines became more accurate as context increased. Security incidents related to privileged misuse declined, not because enforcement intensified, but because understanding improved.

CHAPTER 9

Building Behavioral Intelligence Into Everyday Security Operations

Behavioral intelligence delivers value only when it becomes part of routine security practice. When treated as a specialist capability used occasionally or during investigations, it remains reactive by nature. To influence outcomes meaningfully, behavioral intelligence must be woven into how security teams observe systems, interpret change, and make decisions on a daily basis. This integration requires structural, procedural, and cultural adjustment rather than the introduction of new tools alone.

Most security operations are organized around immediacy. Alerts arrive, tickets are generated, and analysts are expected to respond quickly. This structure encourages event resolution rather than behavioral understanding. Behavioral intelligence operates on a longer timeline. It requires teams to notice how activity evolves across days, weeks, and months. Integrating it into everyday operations means accepting that not all valuable work produces immediate closure. Some of the most important insights emerge slowly through observation and comparison.

A practical starting point is redefining what constitutes operational value. In many environments, productivity is measured by volume: alerts processed, incidents closed, response times improved. Behavioral intelligence introduces a different category of work. Reviewing behavioral trends, correlating activity across systems, and documenting gradual change are tasks that do not fit neatly into traditional metrics. Organizations must recognize these activities as essential to risk management rather than as secondary analysis.

This shift requires changes to workflow design. Behavioral review cannot be squeezed between alert handling without losing depth. Teams need dedicated time to examine behavior outside the pressure of incident response. This often takes the form of scheduled review sessions where analysts step back from queues and focus on how systems are behaving as a whole. These sessions are exploratory rather than directive. The goal is to notice change, raise questions, and record observations, not to resolve incidents.

Tooling should support this mode of work rather than dictate it. Behavioral intelligence does not demand entirely new platforms, but it does require visibility across time and systems. Dashboards that show activity progression, access expansion, and correlation across domains are more valuable than dashboards that highlight individual spikes. Tools should enable analysts to build narratives from data, connecting events into sequences that explain how behavior is changing.

Documentation plays a central role in operationalizing behavioral intelligence. Without documentation, insights are transient. Analysts may recognize behavioral drift, but that understanding disappears when personnel change or attention shifts. Recording why a behavioral pattern was considered benign, concerning, or unresolved creates continuity. This documentation becomes a reference point for future analysis and helps prevent repeated misinterpretation of the same signals.

Behavioral intelligence also requires consistent collaboration with non-security teams. Behavior rarely changes without cause. System owners, developers, and operations teams often hold explanations for observed patterns. Integrating behavioral intelligence into operations means normalizing these conversations. Analysts should feel comfortable asking why behavior has shifted, and system owners should expect to provide context. This exchange reduces speculation and improves accuracy.

Escalation discipline is another operational necessity. Behavioral intelligence generates uncertainty by design. Not every signal demand action. Teams must be comfortable allowing observation to continue when explanations are plausible or when patterns are still forming. Premature escalation disrupts operations and erodes trust. Behavioral intelligence relies on restraint as much as vigilance.

Training is critical to sustaining this approach. Analysts accustomed to event driven response must develop skills in longitudinal analysis and hypothesis testing. They must learn to recognize progression rather than wait for violation. Training programmers should emphasize interpretation, contextual reasoning, and communication alongside technical detection skills. Behavioral intelligence is as much an analytical discipline as a technical one.

Leadership support determines whether these practices endure. Managers must protect time for behavioral analysis and resist pressure to focus exclusively on short term metrics. They must value early understanding even when it does not produce immediate outcomes. Without this support, behavioral intelligence becomes an optional activity that is abandoned during periods of high alert volume.

Over time, embedding behavioral intelligence into everyday operations reshapes security posture. Teams become more familiar with their environments and less dependent on automated alerts. Discussions shift from reacting to incidents toward understanding conditions. Decisions are made with greater context and less urgency. Security operations become steadier, more deliberate, and more informed.

Behavioral intelligence is not a standalone function. It is a way of working. When integrated consistently into daily operations, it changes how security teams see their systems, their users, and their own role. It replaces constant reaction with sustained awareness and allows organizations to manage risk as a developing condition rather than as a sudden event.

9.1 Creating Operational Space for Long-Term Observation

One of the most difficult adjustments organizations must make when integrating behavioral intelligence into daily operations is creating space for long-term observation. Security teams are typically structured around immediacy. Alerts demand attention, incidents require closure, and reporting cycles reinforce short-term focus. In such environments, there is little room for sustained observation. Behavioral intelligence challenges this structure by requiring time that is not immediately productive in traditional terms.

Long-term observation involves reviewing how behavior evolves across extended periods rather than responding to isolated events. This means analysts must be allowed to step away from alert queues to examine trends, correlations, and gradual change. Without protected time, behavioral analysis becomes superficial. Signals are noticed but not explored. Patterns are identified but not interpreted. The value of behavioral intelligence diminishes when it is forced into reactive workflows.

Operational space is not created by adding more tools or staff alone. It requires deliberate scheduling and prioritization. Some organizations establish regular behavioral review sessions where analysts examine access patterns, system usage, and activity progression without the pressure of immediate response. These sessions are not tied to incidents. They are exploratory by design. Their purpose is to surface questions rather than deliver conclusions.

Creating this space also requires redefining performance expectations. Analysts engaged in behavioral review may not close tickets or resolve alerts during that time. Leadership must recognize this as productive work rather than inefficiency. When observation is valued, analysts develop deeper familiarity with systems. They notice subtle shifts that would otherwise be lost. Over time, this familiarity reduces the volume of urgent response by identifying risk earlier.

Without operational space, behavioral intelligence becomes reactive by default. Analysts only engage with behavior once it triggers alerts. The opportunity to recognize early drift is lost. Creating space for observation is therefore not an optional enhancement. It is a foundational requirement for integrating behavioral intelligence into everyday operations.

9.2 Developing Shared Behavioral Language Across Teams

Behavioral intelligence cannot function in isolation. Patterns often span systems owned by different teams, each with its own vocabulary and priorities. Security teams may describe behavior in terms of risk and exposure, while operations teams focus on performance and reliability. Without a shared language, behavioral insights are misunderstood or dismissed. Integrating behavioral intelligence into operations requires deliberate effort to align interpretation across teams.

A shared behavioral language begins with common concepts. Terms such as baseline, drift, escalation, and trajectory must mean the same thing to everyone involved. When security teams describe behavioral drift, system owners should understand that this refers to sustained change without clear explanation, not to blame or error. This clarity reduces defensiveness and encourages cooperation.

Developing shared language also involves framing behavioral analysis in terms that resonate with non-security teams. Instead of presenting alerts or technical anomalies, security teams can describe how usage patterns have changed relative to historical norms. This narrative approach makes behavioral intelligence more accessible and actionable. Conversations shift from justification to understanding.

Regular cross-functional review meetings support this alignment. When teams review behavioral trends together, they develop a shared mental model of how systems behave under normal and stressed conditions. Over time, this shared understanding reduces friction. Explanations are offered proactively. Behavioral baselines become more accurate because context is continuously refined.

Without shared language, behavioral intelligence struggles to gain traction. Signals are interpreted inconsistently, and valuable insights are lost in translation. Developing this language takes time and patience, but it is essential for embedding behavioral intelligence into daily operations. When teams speak about behavior in the same way, prediction, interpretation, and response become coordinated rather than fragmented.

CHAPTER 10

Sustaining Behavioral Intelligence in Complex and Evolving Environments

Behavioral intelligence does not reach a point of completion. Unlike tools that can be deployed and configured once, behavioral intelligence is shaped continuously by how systems, users, and organizations evolve. Environments change in ways that are gradual, uneven, and often undocumented. New applications are introduced, access models shift, teams reorganize, and operational shortcuts become permanent. Sustaining behavioral intelligence requires recognizing that stability is temporary and that behavioral understanding must be actively maintained.

One of the most persistent challenges in sustaining behavioral intelligence is environmental drift. Over time, behaviors that were once exceptions become routine. Temporary permissions remain enabled. Monitoring exclusions accumulate. Workarounds become accepted practice. If behavioral baselines are not reviewed deliberately, they absorb this drift and normalize exposure. Behavioral intelligence loses its sensitivity not because threats disappear, but because change is no longer questioned.

Sustaining behavioral intelligence therefore depends on regular recalibration. Recalibration is not a technical reset. It is an interpretive process. Analysts must examine how behavior has changed and determine whether that change reflects intentional evolution or unmanaged accumulation. This requires historical awareness. Teams must be able to compare present behavior with prior states and understand the decisions that led from one to the other. Without this perspective, recalibration becomes reactive and inconsistent.

Recalibration also requires discipline in documentation. Behavioral intelligence depends on institutional memory. Analysts must record not only what was observed, but why conclusions were reached. When documentation is absent, understanding is lost during team transitions. New analysts inherit data without context and repeat earlier uncertainty. Sustaining behavioral intelligence demands that interpretation be preserved alongside observation.

Organizational change introduces additional complexity. Mergers, restructuring, and leadership shifts alter priorities and workflows. Behavioral intelligence must adapt without being diluted. When security programmers are disrupted by organizational change, behavioral review is often deprioritized in favor of immediate operational needs. Over time, this neglect reduces visibility into how systems are actually being used. Sustaining behavioral intelligence requires continuity even when organizational focus shifts.

Leadership consistency is critical in this regard. Behavioral intelligence cannot be sustained if leadership attention oscillates between prevention and reaction. When incidents dominate discussion, early observation is sidelined. When stability returns, behavioral review may be treated as unnecessary. Sustaining behavioral intelligence requires leadership to value understanding even when no disruption is visible. This consistency reinforces behavioral analysis as a core practice rather than a response to failure.

Tooling sustainability also plays a significant role. Behavioral intelligence relies on data pipelines that span systems and time. As environments evolve, integrations break, logging formats change, and visibility degrades. Sustaining behavioral intelligence requires periodic validation of data quality and coverage. Analysts must confirm that behavioral signals remain representative and that blind spots have not emerged silently. Tools that are not reviewed become sources of false confidence.

Human capability remains the most fragile component. Behavioral intelligence depends on analysts who can interpret ambiguity, recognize progression, and resist premature conclusions. These skills erode without practice. When teams are overwhelmed by alert volume or constrained by rigid workflows, behavioral analysis becomes superficial. Sustaining behavioral intelligence requires protecting analytical capacity and investing in continued skill development.

Training must therefore be ongoing rather than episodic. Analysts must be exposed to evolving behavioral patterns, not just known attack scenarios. They must practice longitudinal analysis and contextual reasoning. Behavioral intelligence is learned through exposure and reflection. Without structured opportunities to develop these skills, teams revert to event based thinking.

Another sustaining challenge is complacency. Successful behavioral intelligence reduces incidents and disruption. This success can paradoxically undermine itself. When environments appear stable, review cycles are shortened, questions are deferred, and assumptions harden. Behavioral intelligence fades quietly. Sustaining it requires intentional resistance to complacency. Teams must continue to observe even when nothing appears wrong.

Sustaining behavioral intelligence also requires accepting its limitations. Behavioral signals will never provide certainty. Patterns may remain ambiguous. Explanations may be incomplete. Organizations must be comfortable operating with probability rather than absolutes. This comfort develops only through consistent practice. When teams trust their interpretive process, uncertainty becomes manageable rather than destabilizing.

Finally, sustaining behavioral intelligence requires recognizing it as a shared responsibility. It cannot belong solely to security teams. System owners, developers, and operational leaders all influence behavior. When behavioral intelligence is embedded across roles, understanding deepens. When it is isolated, insight narrows. Sustaining behavioral intelligence therefore depends on maintaining collaboration and shared accountability.

Behavioral intelligence endures when it is treated as an ongoing discipline rather than a completed initiative. Its strength lies in attention, continuity, and interpretation. In environments defined by complexity and change, these qualities determine whether behavioral intelligence remains a source of clarity or gradually loses relevance.

10.1 Preventing Behavioral Intelligence From Degrading Into Routine Noise

One of the quiet risks in long-term behavioral intelligence programmers is gradual desensitization. When teams observe behavior continuously, patterns that once appeared noteworthy can begin to feel familiar. Over time, analysts may stop questioning certain forms of drift simply because they have been present for long periods without visible consequence.

Behavioral intelligence then loses its edge, not through failure, but through habituation.

Preventing this degradation requires intentional disruption of routine thinking. Teams must periodically challenge their own assumptions about what constitutes normal behavior. This involves revisiting earlier interpretations and asking whether conditions that were once tolerated would still be acceptable if introduced today. Behavioral intelligence thrives when analysts are encouraged to question stability rather than accept it.

Structured review cycles help counteract this tendency. Periodic reassessment of behavioral baselines forces teams to reengage critically with familiar patterns. These reviews should not be limited to technical metrics. They should include discussion of why certain behaviors were previously accepted and whether underlying conditions have changed. Without this reflective process, behavioral intelligence slowly becomes passive monitoring rather than active interpretation.

Rotation of analytical perspective also plays a role. Fresh eyes often notice patterns that long-standing team members overlook. Encouraging peer review of behavioral assessments or rotating analysts through different system domains introduces constructive friction. This friction prevents behavioral intelligence from settling into complacency and keeps interpretation active.

Ultimately, sustaining behavioral intelligence requires ongoing intellectual effort. It demands curiosity even when systems appear stable. When teams continue to question familiar behavior, behavioral intelligence remains a source of insight rather than background noise.

10.2 Maintaining Analytical Rigor as Systems and Threats Evolve

Behavioral intelligence must evolve alongside the environments it protects. As systems become more distributed, automated, and interconnected, behavioral signals change in character. Patterns that were once meaningful may lose relevance, while new forms of interaction introduce unfamiliar risk. Maintaining analytical rigor under these conditions requires deliberate adaptation rather than incremental adjustment.

Analytical rigor begins with understanding how system design influences behavior. Changes in architecture, authentication models, or deployment practices alter how users and services interact. Behavioral intelligence must account for these shifts explicitly. Analysts should examine how design changes affect behavioral baselines rather than assuming continuity. Without this examination, interpretation becomes detached from reality.

Rigor also depends on resisting oversimplification. As environments grow more complex, there is pressure to reduce interpretation to scores or summaries. While abstraction has value, excessive simplification strips away context. Behavioral intelligence requires preserving enough detail to support reasoning. Analysts must remain capable of explaining why a pattern matters, not just that it exists.

Continuous learning supports this rigor. Analysts must stay familiar with evolving technologies, operational practices, and attacker behavior. Behavioral intelligence is weakened when interpretation lags behind environmental change. Training, cross-team collaboration, and exposure to new system domains help maintain analytical sharpness.

Maintaining rigor is ultimately about discipline. Behavioral intelligence does not sustain itself automatically. It requires consistent attention to how behavior is interpreted and why conclusions are reached. When this discipline is preserved, behavioral intelligence remains effective even as systems and threats continue to evolve.

REFERENCES

Anderson, R. (2020). Security engineering: A guide to building dependable distributed systems (3rd ed.). Wiley.

Behl, A., & Behl, K. (2017). Cyberwar: The next threat to national security and what to do about it. Oxford University Press.

Bishop, M. (2018). Computer security: Art and science (2nd ed.). Addison-Wesley.

Buczak, A. L., & Guven, E. (2016). A survey of data mining and machine learning methods for cyber security intrusion detection. IEEE Communications Surveys & Tutorials, 18(2), 1153–1176. https://doi.org/10.1109/COMST.2015.2494502

Casey, E. (2019). Digital evidence and computer crime: Forensic science, computers and the internet (4th ed.). Academic Press.

ENISA. (2018). Machine learning for cybersecurity. European Union Agency for Cybersecurity. https://www.enisa.europa.eu

Garcia-Teodoro, P., Diaz-Verdejo, J., Maciá-Fernández, G., & Vázquez, E. (2009). Anomaly-based network intrusion detection: Techniques, systems and challenges. Computers & Security, 28(1–2), 18–28. https://doi.org/10.1016/j.cose.2008.08.003

Goodfellow, I., McDaniel, P., & Papernot, N. (2018). Making machine learning robust against adversarial inputs. Communications of the ACM, 61(7), 56–66. https://doi.org/10.1145/3134599

NIST. (2018). Framework for improving critical infrastructure cybersecurity (Version 1.1). National Institute of Standards and Technology. https://www.nist.gov

NIST. (2020). Guide to intrusion detection and prevention systems (IDPS) (Special Publication 800-94). National Institute of Standards and Technology. https://doi.org/10.6028/NIST.SP.800-94

Sarker, I. H. (2021). Cybersecurity data science: An overview from machine learning perspective. Journal of Big Data, 8(41). https://doi.org/10.1186/s40537-021-00425-9

Shostack, A. (2014). Threat modeling: Designing for security. Wiley.

Sommer, R., & Paxson, V. (2010). Outside the closed world: On using machine learning for network intrusion detection. IEEE Symposium on Security and Privacy, 305–316. https://doi.org/10.1109/SP.2010.25

Stallings, W., & Brown, L. (2018). Computer security: Principles and practice (4th ed.). Pearson.

Verizon. (2023). Data breach investigations report. Verizon Enterprise. https://www.verizon.com/business/resources/reports/dbir/

www.ingramcontent.com/pod-product-compliance
Lightning Source LLC
Chambersburg PA
CBHW051352240926
51852CB00001B/5
9785376339084